Kaplan Publishing are constantly finding new
looking for exam success and our online reso
extra dimension to your studies.

This book comes with free MyKaplan online r
study anytime, anywhere. **This free online resource is not sold
separately and is included in the price of the book.**

Having purchased this book, you have access to the following online study materials:

CONTENT	AAT	
	Text	Kit
Electronic version of the book	✓	✓
Knowledge Check tests with instant answers	✓	
Mock assessments online	✓	✓
Material updates	✓	✓

How to access your online resources

Received this book as part of your Kaplan course?
If you have a MyKaplan account, your full online resources will be added automatically, in line with the
information in your course confirmation email. If you've not used MyKaplan before, you'll be sent an activation
email once your resources are ready.

Bought your book from Kaplan?
We'll automatically add your online resources to your MyKaplan account. If you've not used MyKaplan before,
you'll be sent an activation email.

Bought your book from elsewhere?
Go to **www.mykaplan.co.uk/add-online-resources**
Enter the ISBN number found on the title page and back cover of this book.
Add the unique pass key number contained in the scratch panel below.
You may be required to enter additional information during this process to set up or confirm your account
details.

This code can only be used once for the registration of this book online. This registration and your online
content will expire when the examinations covered by this book have taken place. Please allow one hour from
the time you submit your book details for us to process your request.

Please scratch the film to access your unique code.

Please be aware that this code is case-sensitive and you will need
to include the dashes within the passcode, but not when entering
the ISBN.

PUBLISHING

AAT

Q2022

Principles of Bookkeeping Controls

EXAM KIT

This Exam Kit supports study for the following AAT qualifications:

AAT Level 2 Certificate in Accounting

AAT Level 2 Certificate in Bookkeeping

AAT Certificate in Accounting at SCQF Level 6

PUBLISHING

British Library Cataloguing-in-Publication Data

A catalogue record for this book is available from the British Library.

Published by:
Kaplan Publishing UK
Unit 2 The Business Centre
Molly Millar's Lane
Wokingham
Berkshire
RG41 2QZ

ISBN: 978-1-83996-580-7

CONTENTS

Features in this exam kit

In addition to providing a wide ranging bank of real exam style questions, we have also included in this kit:

- unit-specific information and advice on exam technique

- our recommended approach to make your revision for this particular unit as effective as possible.

You will find a wealth of other resources to help you with your studies on the AAT website:

www.aat.org.uk/

Quality and accuracy are of the utmost importance to us so if you spot an error in any of our products, please send an email to mykaplanreporting@kaplan.com with full details, or follow the link to the feedback form in MyKaplan.

Our Quality Co-ordinator will work with our technical team to verify the error and take action to ensure it is corrected in future editions.

UNIT-SPECIFIC INFORMATION

THE EXAM

FORMAT OF THE ASSESSMENT

The assessment will comprise eight independent tasks. Students will be assessed by computer-based assessment.

In any one assessment, students may not be assessed on all content, or on the full depth or breadth of a piece of content. The content assessed may change over time to ensure validity of assessment, but all assessment criteria will be tested over time.

The learning outcomes for this unit are as follows:

	Learning outcome	Weighting
1	Use control accounts	25%
2	Reconcile a bank statement with the cash book	25%
3	Use the journal	25%
4	Produce the trial balance	25%
	Total	100%

Time allowed

1½ hours

PASS MARK

The pass mark for all AAT CBAs is 70%.

 Always keep your eye on the clock and make sure you attempt all questions!

DETAILED SYLLABUS

The detailed syllabus and study guide written by the AAT can be found at:

www.aat.org.uk/

INDEX TO QUESTIONS AND ANSWERS

EXAM TECHNIQUE

- **Do not skip any of the material** in the syllabus.

- **Read each question** *very* carefully.

- **Double-check your answer** before committing yourself to it.

- Answer **every** question – if you do not know an answer to a multiple choice question or true/false question, you don't lose anything by guessing. Think carefully before you **guess**.

- If you are answering a multiple-choice question, **eliminate first those answers that you know are wrong.** Then choose the most appropriate answer from those that are left.

- **Don't panic** if you realise you've answered a question incorrectly. Getting one question wrong will not mean the difference between passing and failing.

Computer-based assessments (CBA) – tips

- Do not attempt a CBA until you have **completed all study material** relating to it.

- On the AAT website there is a CBA demonstration. It is **ESSENTIAL** that you attempt this before your real CBA. You will become familiar with how to move around the CBA screens and the way that questions are formatted, increasing your confidence and speed in the actual exam.

- Be sure you understand how to use the **software** before you start the exam. If in doubt, ask the assessment centre staff to explain it to you.

- Questions are **displayed on the screen** and answers are entered using keyboard and mouse. At the end of the exam, you are given a certificate showing the result you have achieved.

- In addition to the traditional multiple-choice question type, CBAs will also contain **other types of questions**, such as number-entry questions, drag and drop, true/false, pick lists or drop down menus or hybrids of these.

- In some CBAs you will have to type in complete computations or written answers.

- You need to be sure you **know how to answer questions** of this type before you sit the exam, through practice.

KAPLAN PUBLISHING

KAPLAN'S RECOMMENDED REVISION APPROACH

QUESTION PRACTICE IS THE KEY TO SUCCESS

Success in professional examinations relies upon you acquiring a firm grasp of the required knowledge at the tuition phase. In order to be able to do the questions, knowledge is essential.

However, the difference between success and failure often hinges on your exam technique on the day and making the most of the revision phase of your studies.

The **Kaplan Study Text** is the starting point, designed to provide the underpinning knowledge to tackle all questions. However, in the revision phase, poring over text books is not the answer.

Kaplan Pocket Notes are designed to help you quickly revise a topic area; however you then need to practise questions. There is a need to progress to exam style questions as soon as possible, and to tie your exam technique and technical knowledge together.

The importance of question practice cannot be over-emphasised.

The recommended approach below is designed by expert tutors in the field, in conjunction with their knowledge of the examiner and the specimen assessment.

You need to practise as many questions as possible in the time you have left.

OUR AIM

Our aim is to get you to the stage where you can attempt exam questions confidently, to time, in a closed book environment, with no supplementary help (i.e. to simulate the real examination experience).

Practising your exam technique is also vitally important for you to assess your progress and identify areas of weakness that may need more attention in the final run up to the examination.

In order to achieve this we recognise that initially you may feel the need to practice some questions with open book help.

Good exam technique is vital.

THE KAPLAN REVISION PLAN

Stage 1: Assess areas of strengths and weaknesses

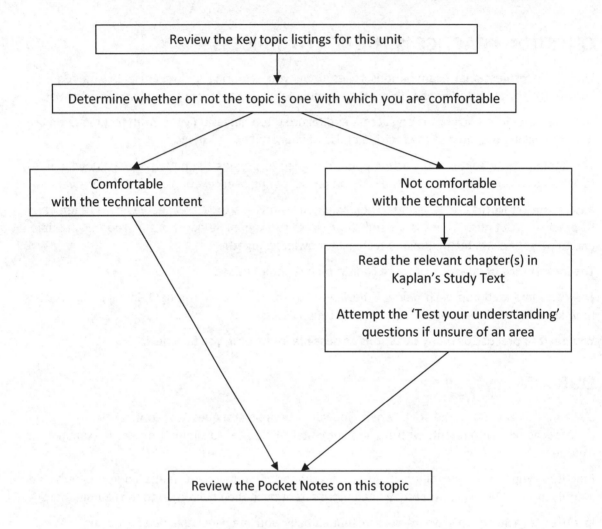

Stage 2: Practise questions

Follow the order of revision of topics as presented in this Kit and attempt the questions in the order suggested.

Try to avoid referring to Study Texts and your notes and the model answer until you have completed your attempt.

Review your attempt with the model answer and assess how much of the answer you achieved.

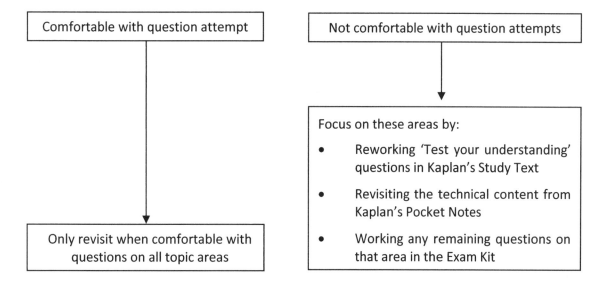

Stage 3: Final pre-exam revision

We recommend that you **attempt at least one mock examination** containing a set of previously unseen exam-standard questions.

Attempt the mock CBA online in timed, closed book conditions to simulate the real exam experience.

Section 1

PRACTICE QUESTIONS

USE CONTROL ACCOUNTS

1   MONSTER MUNCHIES

This is a summary of transactions with customers of Monster Munchies during the month of June.

(a)   **Show whether each entry will be a debit or credit in the Receivables ledger control account in the General ledger.**

Details	Amount £	Debit ✓	Credit ✓
Balance of receivables at 1 June	48,000		
Goods sold on credit	12,415		
Receipts from credit customers	22,513		
Discount allowed	465		
Sales returns from credit customers	320		

(b)   **What will be the balance brought down on 1 July on the above account?**

	✓
Dr £37,117	
Cr £37,117	
Dr £83,713	
Cr £83,713	
Dr £58,883	
Cr £58,883	

The following debit balances were in the subsidiary receivables ledger on 1 July.

	£
XXX Ltd	21,300
Brittle Homes Ltd	5,376
Colin and Campbell	333
Bashford Incorporated	1,733
Mainstreet Homes	3,426
Shamrock Interiors	4,629

(c) **Reconcile the balances shown above with the receivables ledger control account balance you have calculated in part (a).**

	£
Receivables ledger control account balance as at 30 June	
Total of subsidiary receivables ledger accounts as at 30 June	
Difference	

(d) **Which TWO of the following reasons could be explanations of why the total on a receivables ledger control account may be higher than the total of balances on a receivables ledger?**

	✓
Sales returns may have been omitted from the subsidiary ledger.	
Discounts allowed may have been omitted from the subsidiary ledger.	
Sales returns may have been entered in the subsidiary ledger twice.	
Discounts allowed may have been entered in the subsidiary ledger twice.	

It is important to reconcile the receivables ledger control account on a regular basis.

(e) **Which of the following statements is true?**

	✓
Reconciliation of the receivables ledger control account assures managers that the amount showing as owed to suppliers is correct.	
Reconciliation of the receivables ledger control account assures managers that the amount showing as outstanding from customers is correct.	
Reconciliation of the receivables ledger control account will show if a purchase invoice has been omitted from the payables ledger.	
Reconciliation of the receivables ledger control account will show if a purchase invoice has been omitted from the receivables ledger.	

2   **JACK'S BOX**

This is a summary of transactions with customers of Jack's Box during the month of April.

(a)   **Show whether each entry will be a debit or a credit in the Receivables ledger control account in the General ledger.**

Details	Amount £	Debit ✓	Credit ✓
Balance of receivables at 1 April	60,589		
Goods sold on credit	26,869		
Payments received from credit customers	29,411		
Discount allowed	598		
Goods returned from credit customers	1,223		

(b)   **What will be the balance brought down on 1 May on the above account?**

	✓
Dr £55,030	
Cr £55,030	
Dr £56,226	
Cr £56,226	
Dr £52,584	
Cr £52,584	

The following debit balances were in the subsidiary receivables ledger on 1 May.

	£
Olsen & Lane	19,455
Frith Ltd	625
Hodgetts & Co	412
Geevor plc	17,623
Trevaskis Farm Ltd	16,888

(c)   **Reconcile the balances shown above with the receivables ledger control account balance you have calculated in part (b).**

	£
Receivables ledger control account balances as at 30 April	
Total of subsidiary receivables ledger accounts as at 30 April	
Difference	

(d)   What may have caused the difference of £1,223 you calculated in part (c)?

	✓
Sales returns may have been omitted from the subsidiary ledger	
Discounts allowed may have been omitted from the subsidiary ledger	
Sales returns have been entered into the subsidiary ledger twice	
Discounts allowed have been entered into receivables ledger control account twice	

It is important to reconcile the receivables ledger control account on a regular basis.

(e)   Which of the following statements is true?

	✓
Reconciliation of the receivables ledger control account will show if a purchase invoice has been omitted from the payables ledger.	
Reconciliation of the receivables ledger control account will show if a sales invoice has been omitted from the payables ledger.	
Reconciliation of the receivables ledger control account assures managers that the amount showing due to suppliers is correct.	
Reconciliation of the receivables ledger control account assures managers that the amount showing due from customers is correct.	

3   CILLA'S SINKS

This is a summary of transactions with suppliers of Cilla's Sinks during the month of June.

(a)   Show whether each entry will be a debit or credit in the payables ledger control account in the General Ledger.

Details	Amount £	Debit ✓	Credit ✓
Balance of payables at 1 June	52,150		
Goods bought on credit	19,215		
Payments made to credit suppliers	19,073		
Discount received	284		
Goods returned to credit suppliers	1,023		

(b)   **What will be the balance brought down on 1 July on the above account?**

	✓
Dr £51,553	
Cr £51,553	
Dr £50,985	
Cr £50,985	
Dr £50,701	
Cr £50,701	

The following credit balances were in the subsidiary payables ledger on 1 July.

	£
BWF Ltd	19,563
All Parts Ltd	10,207
Hove Albion	4,501
Barton Groves	6,713
Cambridge Irons	5,913
Outside Arenas	5,111

(c)   **Reconcile the balances shown above with the payables ledger control account balance you have calculated in part (a).**

	£
Payables ledger control account balance as at 30 June	
Total of subsidiary payables ledger accounts as at 30 June	
Difference	

It is important to reconcile the payables ledger control account on a regular basis.

(d)   **What may have caused the difference calculated in part (c)?**

	✓
Goods returned may have been omitted from the subsidiary ledger.	
Discounts received may have been omitted from the subsidiary ledger.	
Goods returned may have been entered in the subsidiary ledger twice.	
Discounts received may have been entered into the subsidiary ledger twice.	

(e)   Which of the following statements is true?

	✓
Reconciliation of the payables ledger control account will help to identify any supplier invoices that have been omitted in error.	
Reconciliation of the payables ledger control account will show if a sales invoice has been omitted from the payables ledger.	
Reconciliation of the payables ledger control account will show if a sales invoice has been omitted from the receivables ledger.	
Reconciliation of the payables ledger control account will help to identify any discounts allowed that have been omitted in error.	

4   VIK'S TRICKS

This is a summary of transactions with customers of Vik's Tricks during the month of June.

(a)   Show whether each entry will be a debit or credit in the Receivables ledger control account in the General ledger.

Details	Amount £	Debit ✓	Credit ✓
Balance of receivables at 1 June	58,120		
Goods sold on credit	20,013		
Receipts from credit customers	22,327		
Discount allowed	501		
Sales returns from credit customers	970		

(b)   What will be the balance brought down on 1 July on the above account?

	✓
Dr £58,963	
Cr £58,963	
Dr £57,277	
Cr £57,277	
Dr £54,335	
Cr £54,335	

The following debit balances were in the subsidiary receivables ledger on 1 July.

	£
Woffel Homes	21,026
Perfect Rooms Ltd	14,709
Brighton Dwellings Ltd	7,864
Grosvenor Homes	3,198
Oxford Designs	3,011
Indoor Delights	5,497

(c) **Reconcile the balances shown above with the receivables ledger control account balance you have calculated in part (a).**

	£
Receivables ledger control account balance as at 30 June	
Total of subsidiary receivables ledger accounts as at 30 June	
Difference	

(d) **Which TWO of the following reasons could be explanations of why the total on a receivables ledger control account may be LOWER than the total of balances on a receivables ledger?**

	✓
Discounts allowed may have been entered in the subsidiary ledger twice.	
Discounts allowed may have been omitted from the subsidiary ledger.	
Sales returns may have been entered in the subsidiary ledger twice.	
Sales returns may have been omitted from the subsidiary ledger.	

It is important to reconcile the receivables ledger control account on a regular basis.

(e) **Which of the following statements is true?**

	✓
Reconciliation of the receivables ledger control account will help to identify any customer invoices that have been omitted in error.	
Reconciliation of the receivables ledger control account will show if a purchase invoice has been omitted from the receivables ledger.	
Reconciliation of the receivables ledger control account will show if a purchase invoice has been omitted from the payables ledger.	
Reconciliation of the receivables ledger control account will help to identify any discounts received that have been omitted in error.	

5   ZHANG

When Zhang came to reconcile his RLCA with his list of balances on the receivables ledger, he found that they did not match. The RLCA had a balance of £65,830 and the list of balances totalled £65,090. Upon further investigation, he discovered that the following errors had been made:

1   The sales day book had been incorrectly totalled and had been overcast by £1,200.

2   A contra of £800 had been made in the RLCA, but had not been recorded in the receivables ledger.

3   A credit note of £130 had been posted twice in the receivables ledger.

4   A discount given of £210 had only been recorded in the receivables ledger.

(a)   Update the RLCA and list of balances to make sure that the two agree.

RLCA

Details	Amount £	Details	Amount £
Balance b/d	65,830		
		Balance c/d	
Balance b/d			

List of balances:

	£
Total	65,090
Revised total	

(b)   Show whether the following statements are true or false:

	True ✓	False ✓
An aged trade receivables analysis is used when chasing customers for outstanding payments.		
An aged trade receivables analysis is sent to credit customers when payments are being requested.		

6 HANDYSIDE

When Handyside came to reconcile his PLCA with his list of balances on the payables ledger, he found that they did not match. The PLCA had a balance of £25,360 and the list of balances totalled £26,000. Upon further investigation, he discovered that the following errors had been made:

1 In the payables ledger, a purchase of £2,400 (including VAT at 20%) had been entered at the net amount.

2 Returns of £350 had not been included in the payables ledger.

3 An invoice for £600 plus VAT had not been posted in the PLCA yet.

4 Returns of £120 were missing from the PLCA.

5 An invoice for £340 had been entered into the payables ledger as £430.

(a) **Update the PLCA and list of balances to make sure that the two agree.**

PLCA

Details	Amount £	Details	Amount £
		Balance b/d	25,360
Balance c/d			
		Balance b/d	

List of balances:

	£
Total	26,000
Revised total	

(b) **Show whether the following statements are true or false:**

	True ✓	False ✓
The payables ledger control account enables a business to see how much is owed to individual suppliers		
The payables ledger control account total should reconcile to the total of the list of supplier balances in the payables ledger		

7   RING TELEPHONE

The following is an extract from Ring Telephone's books of prime entry.

		Totals for quarter	
Sales day-book		**Purchases day-book**	
Net:	£153,000	Net:	£81,000
VAT:	£30,600	VAT:	£16,200
Gross:	£183,600	Gross:	£97,200
Sales returns day-book		**Purchases returns day-book**	
Net:	£1,800	Net:	£5,800
VAT:	£360	VAT:	£1,160
Gross:	£2,160	Gross:	£6,960
Cash book			
Net cash sales:	£240		
VAT:	£48		
Gross cash sales:	£288		

(a)   **What will be the entries in the VAT control account to record the VAT transactions in the quarter?**

VAT control

Details	Amount £	Details	Amount £

Picklist: Cash sales, Purchases, Purchases returns, Sales, Sales returns, VAT.

The VAT return has been completed and shows an amount owing from HMRC of £15,248.

(b)   **Is the VAT return correct?**   Yes/No

(c) At the end of the next period, the VAT control account has debit entries amounting to £93,800 and credit entries amounting to £54,400.

The following transactions have not yet been recorded in the VAT control account:

VAT of £400 on purchase of equipment

VAT of £900 on cash sales

What will be the balance brought down on the VAT account after the transactions above have been recorded? Also identify whether the balance will be a debit or a credit.

	£	Debit	Credit
Balance brought down			

8 JO'S JOINERS

The following is an extract from Jo's Joiners books of prime entry.

Totals for quarter			
Sales day book		**Purchases day book**	
Net:	£156,000	Net:	£105,000
VAT:	£31,200	VAT:	£21,000
Gross:	£187,200	Gross:	£126,000
Sales returns day book		**Purchases returns day book**	
Net:	£3,600	Net:	£5,440
VAT:	£720	VAT:	£1,088
Gross:	£4,320	Gross:	£6,528
Cash Book			
Net cash sales:	£600		
VAT:	£120		
Gross cash sales:	£720		

(a) **What will be the entries in the VAT control account to record the VAT transactions in the quarter?**

VAT Control

Details	Amount £	Details	Amount £

Picklist: Cash sales, Purchases, Purchases returns, Sales, Sales returns, VAT.

The VAT return has been completed and shows an amount owed to HMRC of £10,688.

(b) **Is the VAT return correct?** Yes/No

9   KOFI'S KABINS

The following is an extract from Kofi's Kabins books of prime entry.

		Totals for quarter	
Sales day-book		**Purchases day-book**	
Net:	£179,800	Net:	£100,200
VAT:	£35,960	VAT:	£20,040
Gross:	£215,760	Gross:	£120,240
Sales returns day-book		**Purchases returns day-book**	
Net:	£3,000	Net:	£5,720
VAT:	£600	VAT:	£1,144
Gross:	£3,600	Gross:	£6,864
Cash book			
Net cash sales:	£560		
VAT:	£112		
Gross cash sales:	£672		

(a)   **What will be the entries in the VAT control account to record the VAT transactions in the quarter?**

VAT control

Details	Amount £	Details	Amount £

Picklist: Cash sales, Purchases, Purchases returns, Sales, Sales returns, VAT.

The VAT return has been completed and shows an amount due to HMRC of £14,540.

(b)   **Is the VAT return correct?**   Yes/No

10   DISLEY

(a)   Show whether each item is a debit or credit balance in the VAT control account by copying the amount into the correct column.

	£	Debit	Credit
VAT total in the sales day book	65,420		
VAT total in the purchases day book	21,340		
VAT total in the sales returns day book	480		
VAT balance brought forward, owed to HMRC	24,910		
VAT on irrecoverable debts	830		
VAT on petty cash expenses paid	210		

The VAT return has been completed and shows an amount due to HMRC of £67,740.

(b)   **Is the VAT return correct?** Yes/No

(c)   At the end of the next period, the VAT control account has debit entries amounting to £42,300 and credit entries amounting to £61,250.

The following transactions have not yet been recorded in the VAT control account:

VAT total in the discounts received day book of £980

VAT of £200 on an irrecoverable debt

What will be the balance brought down on the VAT account after the transactions above have been recorded? Also identify whether the balance will be a debit or a credit.

	£	Debit	Credit
Balance brought down			

11   KERR

(a)   Show whether each item is a debit or credit balance in the VAT control account by copying the amount into the correct column.

	£	Debit	Credit
VAT total in the purchase returns day book	1,320		
VAT total in discounts received day book	400		
VAT on cash purchases	2,670		
VAT on the sale of equipment	970		
VAT total in discounts allowed day book	500		
VAT refund received from HMRC	2,580		
VAT on cash sales	5,880		
VAT balance brought forward, due from HMRC	2,580		

The VAT return has been completed and shows an amount due to HMRC of £5,400.

(b)   **Is the VAT return correct?** Yes/No

12   NILSSON

(a)   Show whether each item is a debit or credit balance in the VAT control account by copying the amount into the correct column.

	£	Debit	Credit
VAT total in the sales day book	54,670		
VAT total in the purchases day book	26,340		
VAT total in the sales returns day book	1,240		
VAT total in the purchases returns day book	760		
VAT on sale of equipment	3,210		
VAT on petty cash expenses paid	500		
VAT balance brought forward, owed to HMRC	42,180		
VAT on irrecoverable debts	430		
VAT paid to HMRC during the period	32,150		
VAT on cash sales	6,540		
VAT on cash purchases	7,520		
VAT total in discounts allowed day book	1,130		
VAT total in discounts received day book	980		

The VAT return has been completed and shows an amount due to HMRC of £39,030.

(b)   **Is the VAT return correct?** Yes/No

RECONCILE A BANK STATEMENT WITH THE CASH BOOK

13   BLOSSOM BLOOMS

Blossom Blooms receives payment from customers and makes payments to suppliers in a variety of ways.

(a)   Select FOUR checks that DO NOT have to be made on each of the two payment methods shown below when received from customers.

Checks to be made	Cheque ✓	Telephone credit card payment ✓
Check expiry date		
Check issue number		
Check not post dated		
Check security number		
Check words and figures match		
Check card has not been tampered with		

(b) **Show whether each of the statements below is true or false.**

When Blossom Blooms makes payments to suppliers by debit card, the amount paid affects the bank current account.

True/False

When Blossom Blooms makes payments to suppliers by credit card, the amount paid affects the bank current account.

True/False

14   PARI'S PARROTS

Pari's Parrots receives payment from customers and makes payments to suppliers in a variety of ways.

(a) **Select TWO checks that have to be made on each of the two payment methods shown below when received from customers.**

Checks to be made	Cheque ✓	Telephone credit card payment ✓
Check expiry date		
Check issue number		
Check not post dated		
Check security number		
Check words and figures match		
Check card has not been tampered with		

(b) **Show whether each of the statements below is true or false.**

When Pari's Parrots makes payments to suppliers by credit card, the amount does not leave the bank current account immediately.

True/False

When Pari's Parrots makes payments to suppliers by debit card, the amount paid affects the bank current account.

True/False

15   BANK EFFECTS 1

Which TWO payments will NOT reduce funds in the bank balance of the payer at the date of payment?

	✓
Standing order	
Cheque payment	
CHAPS payment	
Credit card payment	

---

16   BANK EFFECTS 2

Which THREE payments WILL reduce funds in the bank balance of the payer at the date of payment?

	✓
Direct debit	
Building society cheque payment	
Debit card payment	
BACS payment	

17   METHODS OF PAYMENT 1

Match the payment need with the most likely method of payment to be used.

Replacement batteries for office clock	CHAPS payment
Payment to complete the purchase of a new building, which needs to clear today	Debit/Credit card
Fixed monthly charge for rent	Direct debit
Payment for telephone bill, which fluctuates monthly	Cheque
Payment to regular supplier	Petty cash
Online purchase of computer equipment	Standing order

18   METHODS OF PAYMENT 2

Match the payment with the description below

Standing order	A payment made for regular bills which fluctuate in value
Bank loan	A facility allowing customers to deposit cash and cheques after bank opening hours
Direct debit	A regular payment for a fixed amount
Bank overdraft	A facility allowing customers to borrow money on a long term basis
Night safe	A facility allowing customers to borrow money on a short term flexible basis

19 RIVERS LTD

The bank statement and cash book of Rivers is shown below.

	Midway Bank PLC				
	52 The Parade, Middleton, MD1 9LA				
To: Rivers Ltd		Account No: 28012877		23 June 20XX	
	Statement of Account				
Date	**Detail**		**Paid out**	**Paid in**	**Balance**
20XX			£	£	£
04 June	Balance b/d				3,115 C
04 June	Cheque 101013		650		2,465 C
04 June	Cheque 101014		1,420		1,045 C
05 June	Cheque 101015		60		985 C
07 June	Cheque 101018		450		535 C
12 June	Bank Giro Credit Ayreshire Build			970	1,505 C
13 June	Cheque 101016		615		890 C
15 June	Direct debit Collins		175		715 C
19 June	Paid in at Midway bank			300	1,015 C
20 June	Direct Debit rent		500		515 C
23 June	Bank interest			15	530 C
23 June	Bank charges		20		510 C
	D = Debit C = Credit				

Cash book

Date 20XX	Details	Bank £	Date 20XX	Cheque number	Details	Bank £
01 June	Balance b/d	3,115	01 June	101013	Indigo Beds	650
17 June	Bracken Ltd	300	01 June	101014	DirectFit	1,420
21 June	Airfleet Interiors	560	01 June	101015	Langdon	60
22 June	Harris Homes	333	02 June	101016	QPF Ltd	615
			03 June	101017	OMD Ltd	815
			03 June	101018	Hamden Ltd	450
			15 June	101019	Freeman and Cope	522
			15 June		Collins	175

Details columns options: Balance b/d, Balance c/d, Bank charges, QPF Ltd, Bracken Ltd, Ayreshire Build, Closing balance, Directfit, Hamden Ltd, Rent, Collins, Langdon, Airfleet Interiors, Freeman and Cope, OMD Ltd, Opening balance, Bank Interest, Indigo Beds, Harris Homes.

(a) Check the items on the bank statement against the items in the cash book.

(b) Enter any items in the cash book as needed.

(c) Total the cash book and clearly show the balance carried down at 23 June (closing balance) and brought down at 24 June (opening balance).

20   LUXURY BATHROOMS

On 28 April Luxury Bathrooms received the following bank statement as at 24 April.

SKB Bank plc				
68 London Road, Reading, RG8 4RN				
To: Luxury Bathrooms	Account No: 55548921		24 April 20XX	
Statement of Account				

Date	Detail	Paid out	Paid in	Balance	
03 April	Balance b/d			17,845	C
03 April	Cheque 120045	8,850		8,995	C
04 April	Bank Giro Credit Ricketts & Co		465	9,460	C
04 April	Cheque 120046	2,250		7,210	C
05 April	Cheque 120047	64		7,146	C
08 April	Cheque 120048	3,256		3,890	C
14 April	Direct Debit AMB Ltd	2,265		1,625	C
14 April	Direct Debit D Draper	2,950		1,325	D
14 April	Cheque 120050	655		1,980	D
22 April	Paid in at SKB bank		2,150	170	C
22 April	Bank charges	63		107	C
23 April	Overdraft fee	25		82	C
D = Debit C = Credit					

The cash book as at 24 April is shown below.

Cash book

Date	Details	Bank	Date	Cheque	Details	Bank
01 April	Balance b/d	17,845	01 April	120045	R Sterling Ltd	8,850
19 April	Olsen & Lane	2,150	01 April	120046	Bert Cooper	2,250
22 April	Frith Ltd	685	01 April	120047	Hetko & Sons	64
22 April	Hodgetts & Co	282	02 April	120048	Barrett Ltd	3,256
			02 April	120049	K Plomer	542
			08 April	120050	I&E Brown	655
			08 April	120051	T Roberts	1,698
			14 April		AMB Ltd	2,265

Details column options: Balance b/d, balance c/d, Bank charges, R Sterling Ltd, Olsen & Lane, Frith Ltd, Hodgetts & Co, Bert Cooper, Hetko & Sons, Barrett Ltd, K Plomer, I&E Brown, T Roberts, AMB Ltd, Ricketts & Co, D Draper, Opening balance, Overdraft fees.

(a)   **Check the items on the bank statement against the items in the cash book.**

(b)   **Enter any items in the cash book as needed.**

(c)   **Total the cash book and clearly show the balance carried down at 24 April (closing balance) and brought down at 25 April (opening balance).**

21 WHOLESALE FLOORING

The bank statement and cash book for Wholesale Flooring is shown below.

Money Bags Bank PLC				
52 Oak Road, Timperley, SK10 8LR				
To: Wholesale Flooring	Account No: 47013799		23 June 20XX	

Statement of Account

Date	Detail	Paid out	Paid in	Balance	
20XX		£	£	£	
04 June	Balance b/d			5,125	D
05 June	Cheque 104373	890		6,015	D
05 June	Cheque 104374	1,725		7,740	D
05 June	Cheque 104375	210		7,950	D
11 June	Cheque 104378	784		8,734	D
12 June	Bank Giro Credit Aintree and Co		1,250	7,484	D
13 June	Cheque 104376	1,275		8,759	D
15 June	Cheque 104377	725		9,484	D
17 June	Paid in at Money Bags Bank plc		550	8,934	D
20 June	Direct debit MD County Council	400		9,334	D
23 June	Bank charges	160		9,494	D
23 June	Overdraft fee	90		9,584	D
	D = Debit C = Credit				

Cash book

Date 20XX	Details	Bank £	Date 20XX	Cheque number	Details	Bank £
			01 June		Balance b/d	5,125
16 June	Beeston's	550	01 June	104373	Good Iron	890
19 June	Airfleet Exteriors	3,025	01 June	104374	Ashworth & Co	1,725
22 June	Jones's	2,775	01 June	104375	Ironfit	210
			05 June	104376	OSS Ltd	1,275
			07 June	104377	Perfect Tools	725
			08 June	104378	Campden Ltd	784
			14 June	104379	Thornley & Thwaite	675
			14 June	104380	Castle & Cove	178

Details columns options: Balance b/d, Balance c/d, Bank charges, Good Iron, Beeston's, Aintree & Co, Perfect Tools, Closing balance, Ashworth & Co, Thornley & Thwaite, MD County Council, Campden Ltd, Airfleet Exteriors, Castle & Cove, OSS Ltd, Opening balance, Overdraft Fee, Ironfit, Jones's.

(a)   **Check the items on the bank statement against the items in the cash book.**

(b)   **Enter any items in the cash book as needed.**

(c)   **Total the cash book and clearly show the balance carried down at 23 June (closing balance) and brought down at 24 June (opening balance).**

22   24 HOUR TAXIS

On 28 June 24 Hour Taxis received the following bank statement as at 23 June.

	Four Kings Bank PLC 124 Four Kings Way, Newton Mearns, GL10 5QR			
To: 24 Hour Taxis	Account No: 16135844			23 June 20XX

Statement of Account

Date 20XX	Detail	Paid out £	Paid in £	Balance £	
04 June	Balance b/d			6,025	C
05 June	Cheque 102597	910		5,115	C
05 June	Cheque 102598	2,010		3,105	C
05 June	Cheque 102599	315		2,790	C
11 June	Cheque 102602	675		2,115	C
12 June	Bank Giro Credit Barron Homes		1,475	3,590	C
13 June	Cheque 102600	1,725		1,865	C
15 June	Cheque 102601	686		1,179	C
17 June	Paid in at Four Kings Bank		1,000	2,179	C
20 June	Direct Debit AB Insurance	1,250		929	C
23 June	Bank charges	50		879	C
23 June	Overdraft fee	25		854	C
	D = Debit C = Credit				

Cash book

Date 20XX	Details	Bank £	Date 20XX	Cheque number	Details	Bank £
01 June	Balance b/d	6,025	01 June	102597	Best Ideas	910
18 June	Earnshaw's	1,000	02 June	102598	Bentley & Burn	2,010
19 June	Mainstreet Ltd	1,206	02 June	102599	Bits & Bats	315
21 June	Housley Inc	1,725	03 June	102600	LPF Ltd	1,725
			07 June	102601	Essentials	686
			08 June	102602	Hopburn Ltd	675
			15 June	102603	Thistle Tools	410
			15 June	102604	C Campbell Ltd	275

Details columns options: Balance b/d, Balance c/d, Bank charges, Earnshaw's, Housley Inc, C Campbell Ltd, Mainstreet Ltd, Closing balance, Barron Homes, Thistle Tools, AB Insurance, Hopburn Ltd, Best Ideas, Bentley & Burn, LPF Ltd, Opening balance, Overdraft Fee, Bits & Bats, Essentials.

(a)   Check the items on the bank statement against the items in the cash book.

(b)   Enter any items in the cash book as needed.

(c)   Total the cash book and clearly show the balance carried down at 23 June (closing balance) and brought down at 24 June (opening balance).

23 WOOD

The bank statement and cash book for Wood is shown below.

Money Bags Bank PLC
52 Oak Road, Timperley, SK10 8LR

To: Wood Ltd	Account No: 47013799	23 June 20XX

Statement of Account

Date 20XX	Detail	Paid out £	Paid in £	Balance £	
04 June	Balance b/d			17,640	C
05 June	Bank Giro Credit Bradley		1,320	18,960	C
05 June	Bank Giro Credit Thanoj		2,450	21,410	C
05 June	Paid in at Money Bags Bank PLC		9,420	30,830	C
11 June	Cheque 110341	1,540		29,290	C
12 June	BACS payment Southwell	820		28,470	C
13 June	Cheque 110343	750		27,720	C
15 June	Cheque 110344	570		27,150	C
17 June	Interest earned		80	27,230	C
20 June	Direct debit Blundell	400		26,830	C
23 June	BACS payment Bore	250		26,580	C
23 June	Cheque 110346	740		25,840	C
	D = Debit C = Credit				

Cash book

Date 20XX	Details	Bank £	Date 20XX	Cheque number	Details	Bank £
01 June	Balance b/d	17,640				
03 June	Bradley	1,320	04 June	110341	Carr	1,540
03 June	Cash sales	9,420	04 June	110342	Ramsden	980
03 June	Thanoj	2,450	04 June	110343	Coulson	750
21 June	Cash sales	7,430	04 June	110344	Brodie	570
21 June	Devitt	1,990	04 June	110345	Jones	550
			04 June	110346	Gritton	740
			20 June		Bore	250

(a) Check the items on the bank statement against the items in the cash book.

(b) Enter any items in the cash book as needed.

(c) Total the cash book and clearly show the balance carried down at 23 June (closing balance) and brought down at 24 June (opening balance).

24   CHANG

The bank statement and cash book for Chang is shown below:

	Money Bags Bank PLC				
To: Chang Ltd		Account No: 47013799		23 June 20XX	
	Statement of Account				
Date	**Detail**	**Paid out**	**Paid in**	**Balance**	
20XX		£	£	£	
01 June	Balance b/d			1,340	D
02 June	Bank Giro Credit Pond		1,890	550	C
02 June	Interest received		5	555	C
02 June	Direct Debit McMenemy	1,200		645	D
11 June	Cheque 110123	430		1,075	D
12 June	Paid in to Money Bags Bank		840	235	D
13 June	Cheque 110126	75		310	D
15 June	Cheque 110127	270		580	D
17 June	Paid in to Money Bags Bank		1,540	960	C
20 June	Direct debit Findus	300		660	C
23 June	Bank charges	25		635	C
23 June	Cheque 110129	740		105	D
	D = Debit C = Credit				

Cash book

Date 20XX	Details	Bank £	Date 20XX	Cheque number	Details	Bank £
01 June	Balance b/d	550	07 June	110123	Connell	430
09 June	Cash sales	840	07 June	110124	Renner	720
14 June	Cash sales	1,540	07 June	110125	Bond	750
22 June	Cunnington	1,730	07 June	110126	Hatton	75
			07 June	110127	Bull	270
			07 June	110128	Black	135
			07 June	110129	Southall	740

(a)   Check the items on the bank statement against the items in the cash book.

(b)   Enter any items in the cash book as needed.

(c)   Total the cash book and clearly show the balance carried down at 23 June (closing balance) and brought down at 24 June (opening balance).

25   MCKEOWN

The bank statement and cash book for McKeown is shown below.

	Money Bags Bank PLC					
To: McKeown Ltd	Account No: 47013799			23 June 20XX		
	Statement of Account					
Date	**Detail**		**Paid out**	**Paid in**	**Balance**	
20XX			£	£	£	
01 June	Balance b/d				7,420	C
01 June	Bank Giro Credit Pond			180	7,600	C
01 June	Cheque 110156		420		7,180	C
01 June	Interest received			85	7,265	C
11 June	Cheque 110157		430		6,835	C
12 June	Cheque 110158		520		6,315	C
13 June	Cheque 110161		750		5,565	C
15 June	Bank Giro Credit Sherwood			640	6,205	C
17 June	Paid in to Money Bags Bank			1,200	7,405	C
20 June	Bank Giro Credit Coyne			1,630	9,035	C
23 June	Direct debit Wilmott		300		8,735	C
23 June	Interest received			35	8,770	C
	D = Debit C = Credit					

Cash book

Date 20XX	Details	Bank £	Date 20XX	Cheque number	Details	Bank £
01 June	Balance b/d	7,180	07 June	110157	Williams	430
12 June	Sherwood	640	07 June	110158	Forecast	520
14 June	Cash sales	1,200	07 June	110159	Beasant	1,240
22 June	Tweedy	860	07 June	110160	Davison	1,420
23 June	Butterwood	440	07 June	110161	Mildenhall	750

(a)   Check the items on the bank statement against the items in the cash book.

(b)   Enter any items in the cash book as needed.

(c)   Total the cash book and clearly show the balance carried down at 23 June (closing balance) and brought down at 24 June (opening balance).

26   RIVERS BANK RECONCILIATION

Below is the bank statement and updated cash book for Rivers.

<table>
<tr><td colspan="6" align="center">**Midway Bank PLC**
52 The Parade, Middleton, MD1 9LA</td></tr>
<tr><td colspan="2">To: Rivers Ltd</td><td colspan="2" align="center">Account No: 28012877</td><td colspan="2" align="right">23 June 20XX</td></tr>
<tr><td colspan="6" align="center">**Statement of Account**</td></tr>
<tr><td>**Date**</td><td>**Detail**</td><td>**Paid out**</td><td>**Paid in**</td><td>**Balance**</td><td></td></tr>
<tr><td>**20XX**</td><td></td><td>£</td><td>£</td><td>£</td><td></td></tr>
<tr><td>04 June</td><td>Balance b/d</td><td></td><td></td><td>3,115</td><td>C</td></tr>
<tr><td>04 June</td><td>Cheque 101013</td><td>650</td><td></td><td>2,465</td><td>C</td></tr>
<tr><td>04 June</td><td>Cheque 101014</td><td>1,420</td><td></td><td>1,045</td><td>C</td></tr>
<tr><td>05 June</td><td>Cheque 101015</td><td>60</td><td></td><td>985</td><td>C</td></tr>
<tr><td>07 June</td><td>Cheque 101018</td><td>450</td><td></td><td>535</td><td>C</td></tr>
<tr><td>12 June</td><td>Bank Giro Credit Ayreshire Build</td><td></td><td>970</td><td>1,505</td><td>C</td></tr>
<tr><td>13 June</td><td>Cheque 101016</td><td>615</td><td></td><td>890</td><td>C</td></tr>
<tr><td>15 June</td><td>Direct debit Collins</td><td>175</td><td></td><td>715</td><td>C</td></tr>
<tr><td>17 June</td><td>Paid in at Midway bank</td><td></td><td>300</td><td>1,015</td><td>C</td></tr>
<tr><td>20 June</td><td>Direct Debit rent</td><td>500</td><td></td><td>515</td><td>C</td></tr>
<tr><td>23 June</td><td>Bank interest</td><td></td><td>15</td><td>530</td><td>C</td></tr>
<tr><td>23 June</td><td>Bank charges</td><td>20</td><td></td><td>510</td><td>C</td></tr>
<tr><td colspan="6" align="center">D = Debit   C = Credit</td></tr>
</table>

Date 20XX	Details	Bank £	Date 20XX	Cheque number	Details	Bank £
01 June	Balance b/d	3,115	01 June	101013	Indigo Beds	650
17 June	Bracken Ltd	300	01 June	101014	DirectFit	1,420
21 June	Airfleet Interiors	560	01 June	101015	Langdon	60
22 June	Harris Homes	333	01 June	101016	QPF Ltd	615
12 June	Ayreshire Build	970	02 June	101017	OMD Ltd	815
23 June	Bank Interest	15	02 June	101018	Hamden Ltd	450
			13 June	101019	Freeman & Cope	522
			13 June		Collins	175
			20 June		Rent	500
			23 June		Bank charges	20
			23 June		Balance c/d	66
		5,293				5,293
24 June	Balance b/d	66				

Complete the bank reconciliation statement as at 23 June.

Note: Do not make any entries in the shaded boxes.

Bank reconciliation statement as at 23 June 20XX

Balance per bank statement	£
Add:	
Name:	£
Name:	£
Total to add	£
Less:	
Name:	£
Name:	£
Total to subtract	£
Balance as per cash book	£

Name options: Bank charges, QPF Ltd, Bracken Ltd, Ayreshire Build, Directfit, Hamden Ltd, Rent, Collins, Langdon, Airfleet Interiors, Freeman and Cope, OMD Ltd, Bank interest, Indigo Beds, Harris homes.

27 LUXURY BATHROOMS BANK RECONCILIATION

Below is the bank statement and updated cash book for Luxury Bathrooms.

	SKB Bank plc					
	68 London Road, Reading, RG8 4RN					
To: Luxury Bathrooms	Account No: 55548921			24 April 20XX		
	Statement of Account					
Date	Detail		Paid out	Paid in	Balance	
20XX			£	£	£	
03 April	Balance b/d				17,845	C
03 April	Cheque 120045		8,850		8,995	C
04 April	Bank Giro Ricketts & Co			465	9,460	C
04 April	Cheque 120046		2,250		7,210	C
05 April	Cheque 120047		64		7,146	C
08 April	Cheque 120048		3,256		3,890	C
14 April	Direct Debit AMB Ltd		2,265		1,625	C
14 April	Direct Debit D Draper		2,950		1,325	D
14 April	Cheque 120050		655		1,980	D
22 April	Paid in at SKB Bank			2,150	170	C
22 April	Bank charges		63		107	C
23 April	Overdraft fee		25		82	C
	D = Debit C = Credit					

Date	Details	Bank	Date	Cheque	Details	Bank
01 April	Balance b/d	17,845	01 April	120045	R Sterling Ltd	8,850
19 April	Olsen & Lane	2,150	01 April	120046	Bert Cooper	2,250
22 April	Frith Ltd	685	01 April	120047	Hetko & Sons	64
22 April	Hodgetts & Co	282	02 April	120048	Barrett Ltd	3,256
04 April	Ricketts & Co	465	02 April	120049	K Plomer	542
			08 April	120050	I&E Brown	655
			08 April	120051	T Roberts	1,698
			14 April		AMB Ltd	2,265
			14 April		D Draper	2,950
			22 April		Bank charges	63
			23 April		Overdraft fee	25
24 April	Balance c/d	1,191				
		22,618				22,618
			25 April		Balance b/d	1,191

Complete the bank reconciliation statement as at 24 April.

Note: Do not make any entries in the shaded boxes.

Bank reconciliation statement as at 24 April 20XX.

Balance per bank statement	£
Add:	
Name:	£
Name:	£
Total to add	£
Less:	
Name:	£
Name:	£
Total to subtract	£
Balance as per cash book	£

Name options: Bank charges, , R Sterling Ltd, Olsen & Lane, Frith Ltd, Hodgetts & Co, Bert Cooper, Hetko & Sons, Barrett Ltd, K Plomer, I&E Brown, T Roberts, AMB Ltd, Ricketts & Co, D Draper, Overdraft fee.

28   WHOLESALE FLOORING BANK RECONCILIATION

Below is the bank statement and updated cash book for Wholesale Flooring.

Money Bags Bank PLC
52 Oak Road, Timperley, SK10 8LR

To: Wholesale Flooring   Account No: 47013799   23 June 20XX

Statement of Account

Date	Detail	Paid out	Paid in	Balance	
20XX		£	£	£	
04 June	Balance b/d			5,125	D
05 June	Cheque 104373	890		6,015	D
05 June	Cheque 104374	1,725		7,740	D
05 June	Cheque 104375	210		7,950	D
11 June	Cheque 104378	784		8,734	D
12 June	Bank Giro Credit Aintree and Co		1,250	7,484	D
13 June	Cheque 104376	1,275		8,759	D
15 June	Cheque 104377	725		9,484	D
17 June	Paid in at Money Bags Bank plc		550	8,934	D
20 June	Direct debit MD County Council	400		9,334	D
23 June	Bank charges	160		9,494	D
23 June	Overdraft fee	90		9,584	D
	D = Debit C = Credit				

Date 20XX	Details	Bank £	Date 20XX	Cheque number	Details	Bank £
			01 June		Balance b/d	5,125
16 June	Beeston's	550	01 June	104373	Good Iron	890
19 June	Airfleet Exteriors	3,025	01 June	104374	Ashworth & Co	1,725
22 June	Jones's	2,775	01 June	104375	Ironfit	210
12 June	Aintree & Co	1,250	05 June	104376	OSS Ltd	1,275
			07 June	104377	Perfect Tools	725
			08 June	104378	Campden Ltd	784
			14 June	104379	Thornley & Thwaite	675
			14 June	104380	Castle and Cove	178
			20 June		MD County Council	400
			23 June		Bank charges	160
23 June	Balance c/d	4,637	23 June		Overdraft fee	90
		12,237				12,237
			24 June		Balance b/d	4,637

Complete the bank reconciliation statement as at 23 June.

Note: Do not make any entries in the shaded boxes.

Bank reconciliation statement as at 23 June 20XX

Balance per bank statement	£
Add:	
Name:	£
Name:	£
Total to add	£
Less:	
Name:	£
Name:	£
Total to subtract	£
Balance as per cash book	£

Name options: Bank charges, OSS Ltd, Beeston's, Aintree and Co, Ironfit, Campden Ltd, MD County Council, Ashworth & Co, Airfleet Exteriors, Thornley & Thwaite, Perfect Tools, Overdraft fee, Castle & Cove, Good Iron, Jones's.

29 24 HOUR TAXIS BANK RECONCILIATION

Below is the bank statement and updated cash book for 24 Hour Taxis.

Four Kings Bank PLC
124 Four Kings Way, Newton Mearns, GL10 5QR

To: 24 Hour Taxis		Account No: 16135844		23 June 20XX	
		Statement of Account			
Date	**Detail**	**Paid out**	**Paid in**	**Balance**	
20XX		£	£	£	
04 June	Balance b/d			6,025	C
05 June	Cheque 102597	910		5,115	C
05 June	Cheque 102598	2,010		3,105	C
05 June	Cheque 102599	315		2,790	C
11 June	Cheque 102602	675		2,115	C
12 June	Bank Giro credit Barron Homes		1,475	3,590	C
13 June	Cheque 102600	1,725		1,865	C
15 June	Cheque 102601	686		1,179	C
18 June	Paid in at Four Kings Bank		1,000	2,179	C
20 June	Direct Debit AB Insurance	1,250		929	C
23 June	Bank charges	50		879	C
23 June	Overdraft fee	25		854	C
	D = Debit C = Credit				

Date 20XX	Details	Bank £	Date 20XX	Cheque number	Details	Bank £
01 June	Balance b/d	6,025	01 June	102597	Best ideas	910
18 June	Earnshaw's	1,000	02 June	102598	Bentley and Burn	2,010
19 June	Mainstreet Ltd	1,206	02 June	102599	Bits and Bats	315
21 June	Housley Inc	1,725	03 June	102600	LPF Ltd	1,725
12 June	Barron Homes	1,475	07 June	102601	Essentials	686
			08 June	102602	Hopburn Ltd	675
			15 June	102603	Thistle Tools	410
			15 June	102604	C Campbell Ltd	275
			20 June		AB Insurance	1,250
			23 June		Bank charges	50
			23 June		Overdraft fee	25
			23 June		Balance c/d	3,100
		11,431				11,431
24 June	Balance b/d	3,100				

Complete the bank reconciliation statement as at 23 June.

Note: Do not make any entries in the shaded boxes.

Bank reconciliation statement as at 23 June 20XX

Balance per bank statement	£
Add:	
Name:	£
Name:	£
Total to add	£
Less:	
Name:	£
Name:	£
Total to subtract	£
Balance as per cash book	£

Name options: Bank charges, LPF Ltd, Earnshaw's, Barron Homes, Best Ideas, C Campbell Ltd, AB Insurance, Housley Inc, Mainstreet Ltd, Thistle Tools, Bentley and Burn, Overdraft fee, Hopburn Ltd, Bits & Bats, Essentials.

30   WOOD BANK RECONCILIATION

The bank statement and cash book for Wood is shown below.

Money Bags Bank PLC					
52 Oak Road, Timperley, SK10 8LR					

To: Wood Ltd   Account No: 47013799   23 June 20XX

Statement of Account

Date 20XX	Detail	Paid out £	Paid in £	Balance £	
04 June	Balance b/d			17,640	C
05 June	Bank Giro Credit Bradley		1,320	18,960	C
05 June	Bank Giro Credit Thanoj		2,450	21,410	C
05 June	Paid in at Money Bags Bank PLC		9,420	30,830	C
11 June	Cheque 110341	1,540		29,290	C
12 June	BACS payment Southwell	820		28,470	C
13 June	Cheque 110343	750		27,720	C
15 June	Cheque 110344	570		27,150	C
17 June	Interest earned		80	27,230	C
20 June	Direct Debit Blundell	400		26,830	C
23 June	BACS payment Bore	250		26,580	C
23 June	Cheque 110346	740		25,840	C

D = Debit   C = Credit

Cash book

Date 20XX	Details	Bank £	Date 20XX	Cheque number	Details	Bank £
01 June	Balance b/d	17,640				
03 June	Bradley	1,320	04 June	110341	Carr	1,540
03 June	Cash sales	9,420	04 June	110342	Ramsden	980
03 June	Thanoj	2,450	04 June	110343	Coulson	750
21 June	Cash sales	7,430	04 June	110344	Brodie	570
21 June	Devitt	1,990	04 June	110345	Jones	550
17 June	Interest earned	80	04 June	110346	Gritton	740
			20 June		Bore	250
			12 June		Southwell	820
			20 June		Direct Debit Blundell	400

                                                                                      KAPLAN PUBLISHING

(a) Complete the bank reconciliation statement as at 23 June.

Note: Do not make any entries in the shaded boxes.

Bank reconciliation statement as at 23 June 20XX

Balance per bank statement	
Add:	
Name:	
Name:	
Total to add	
Less:	
Name:	
Name:	
Total to subtract	
Balance as per cash book	

(b) Refer to the cash book in (a) and check that the bank statement has correctly been reconciled by calculating:

- The balance carried down

- The total of each of the bank columns after the balance carried down has been recorded

Balance carried down	Bank column totals
£	£

31 CHANG BANK RECONCILIATION

The bank statement and cash book for Chang is shown below.

Money Bags Bank PLC					
To: Chang Ltd	Account No: 47013799			23 June 20XX	
Statement of Account					
Date	**Detail**	**Paid out**	**Paid in**	**Balance**	
20XX		£	£	£	
01 June	Balance b/d			1,340	D
02 June	Bank Giro Credit Pond		1,890	550	C
02 June	Interest received		5	555	C
02 June	Direct Debit McMenemy	1,200		645	D
11 June	Cheque 110123	430		1,075	D
12 June	Paid in to Money Bags Bank		840	235	D
13 June	Cheque 110126	75		310	D
15 June	Cheque 110127	270		580	D
17 June	Paid in to Money Bags bank		1,540	960	C
20 June	Direct Debit Findus	300		660	C
23 June	Bank charges	25		635	C
23 June	Cheque 110129	740		105	D
D = Debit C = Credit					

Cash book

Date 20XX	Details	Bank £	Date 20XX	Cheque number	Details	Bank £
01 June	Balance b/d	550	07 June	110123	Connell	430
09 June	Cash sales	840	07 June	110124	Renner	720
14 June	Cash sales	1,540	07 June	110125	Bond	750
22 June	Cunnington	1,730	07 June	110126	Hatton	75
02 June	Interest received	5	07 June	110127	Bull	270
			07 June	110128	Black	135
			07 June	110129	Southall	740
			02 June		McMenemy	1,200
			20 June		Findus	300
			23 June		Bank charges	25
			23 June		Balance c/d	20
		4,665				4,665
24 June	Balance b/d	20				

(a)   **Complete the bank reconciliation statement as at 23 June.**

Note: Do not make any entries in the shaded boxes.

Bank reconciliation statement as at 23 June 20XX

Balance per bank statement	
Add:	
Name:	
Total to add	
Less:	
Name:	
Name:	
Name:	
Total to subtract	
Balance as per cash book	

(b)   **Show which security procedure listed below Chang should use to ensure the security of receipts from customers.**

	✓
Cash received from customers should be kept in a locked safe until banked	
Cash should be banked on a monthly basis	
Cheques received too late to bank should be posted through the bank's letter box	

32   MCKEOWN BANK RECONCILIATION

The bank statement and cash book for McKeown is shown below.

Money Bags Bank PLC

To: McKeown Ltd   Account No: 47013799   23 June 20XX

Statement of Account

Date	Detail	Paid out	Paid in	Balance	
20XX		£	£	£	
01 June	Balance b/d			7,420	C
01 June	Bank Giro Credit Pond		180	7,600	C
01 June	Cheque 110156	420		7,180	C
01 June	Interest received		85	7,265	C
11 June	Cheque 110157	430		6,835	C
12 June	Cheque 110158	520		6,315	C
13 June	Cheque 110161	750		5,565	C
15 June	Bank Giro Credit Sherwood		640	6,205	C
17 June	Paid in to Money Bags Bank		1,200	7,405	C
20 June	Bank Giro Credit Coyne		1,630	9,035	C
23 June	Direct Debit Wilmott	300		8,735	C
23 June	Interest received		35	8,770	C
	D = Debit C = Credit				

Cash book

Date 20XX	Details	Bank £	Date 20XX	Cheque number	Details	Bank £
01 June	Balance b/d	7,180	07 June	110157	Williams	430
12 June	Sherwood	640	07 June	110158	Forecast	520
14 June	Cash sales	1,200	07 June	110159	Beasant	1,240
22 June	Tweedy	860	07 June	110160	Davison	1,420
23 June	Butterwood	440	07 June	110161	Mildenhall	750
01 June	Interest received	85	23 June		Wilmott	300
20 June	Coyne	1,630				
23 June	Interest received	35				

(a) Complete the bank reconciliation statement as at 23 June.

Note: Do not make any entries in the shaded boxes.

Bank reconciliation statement as at 23 June 20XX

Balance per bank statement	
Add:	
Name:	
Name:	
Total to add	
Less:	
Name:	
Name:	
Total to subtract	
Balance as per cash book	

(b) Refer to the cash book in (a) and check that the bank statement has correctly been reconciled by calculating:

– the balance carried down

– the total of each of the bank columns after the balance carried down has been recorded.

Balance carried down £	Bank column totals £

USE THE JOURNAL

33   INTREPID INTERIORS

(a)   Intrepid Interiors has started a new business, Intrepid Exteriors, and a new set of accounts are to be opened. A partially completed journal to record the opening entries is shown below.

Record the journal entries needed in the accounts in the general ledger of Intrepid Exteriors to deal with the opening entries.

Account name	Amount £	Debit ✓	Credit ✓
Cash at bank	7,250		
Bank loan	5,000		
Capital	10,625		
Motor vehicles	4,750		
Insurances	575		
Stationery	300		
Sundry expenses	225		
Motor expenses	135		
Advertising	990		
Rent and rates	1,400		
Journal to record the opening entries of new business			

(b)   **From the list below, select which one of the following transactions would be recorded in the journal.**

Picklist: Credit sale, contra, electricity expense, reimbursement of petty cash

34   BITSY CAKES

(a)   Record the journal entries needed in the accounts in the general ledger of Bitsy Cakes to show if each item is a debit or credit.

Account name	Amount £	Debit ✓	Credit ✓
Cash	325		
Cash at bank	9,625		
Capital	22,008		
Fixtures and fittings	4,250		
Insurance	1,050		
Loan from bank	15,000		
Miscellaneous expenses	413		
Motor vehicle	19,745		
Office expenses	350		
Rent and rates	1,250		

(b)   From the list below, select which one of the following transactions would be recorded in the journal.

Picklist: Prompt payment discount given, the return of goods to a supplier, interest received from the bank, irrecoverable debt written off

35   GARAM GARDENS

Record the journal entries in the general ledger of Garam Gardens to show if each item is a debit or a credit

Account name	Amount £	Debit ✓	Credit ✓
Cash	450		
Cash at bank	11,125		
Capital	26,248		
Plant and machinery	5,050		
Insurance	990		
Loan from bank	12,500		
General office expenses	378		
Motor vehicle	20,755		

36 IVANO

Ivano's pay details for June are listed below:

Transaction	Amount £
Gross pay	2,400
PAYE	480
Employee's NIC	245
Employee's contribution to pension	80
Employer's NIC	255

Fill in the boxes required below:

(a)

	Amount £
Net pay	

(b)

	Amount £
Wages and salaries (Employer's expense)	

(c)

	Amount £
Liabilities (HMRC and pension)	

37 ANNA

Anna's pay details for June are listed below:

Transaction	Amount £
Gross pay	1,400
PAYE	280
Employee's NIC	125
Employer's contribution to pension	70
Employee's contribution to pension	60
Employer's NIC	135

Fill in the boxes required below:

(a)

	Amount £
Net pay	

(b)

	Amount £
Wages and salaries (Employer's expense)	

(c)

	Amount £
Liabilities (HMRC and pension)	

38   GROSS PAY 1

Which of the items listed below would be added to an employee's gross pay to calculate the total wages expense?

Item	Added to gross pay ✓	Not added to gross pay ✓
Trade Union subscription		
Employer's NIC		
Employee's Pension		
Employer's Pension		
Employee's NIC		

39   GROSS PAY 2

Which of the items listed below would be deducted from an employee's gross pay to calculate net pay?

Item	Deducted from gross pay ✓	Not deducted from gross pay ✓
Employer's NIC		
Commission		
Employee's NIC		
Employee pension contribution		
PAYE		

40   A POCKET FULL OF POSES

A Pocket Full of Poses pays its employees by cheque every month and maintains a wages control account. A summary of last month's payroll transactions is shown below:

Item	£
Gross wages	15,000
Employers' NI	1,755
Employees' NI	1,410
Income tax	4,335
Employers' pension contributions	1,000
Employees' pension contributions	850

Record the journal entries needed in the general ledger to:

(i)   Record the wages expense

(ii)   Record the HMRC liability

(iii) Record the net wages paid to the employees

(iv) Record the pension liability.

(i)

Account name	Amount £	Debit ✓	Credit ✓

(ii)

Account name	Amount £	Debit ✓	Credit ✓

(iii)

Account name	Amount £	Debit ✓	Credit ✓

(iv)

Account name	Amount £	Debit ✓	Credit ✓

Picklist for each: Bank, Employees NI, Employers NI, HMRC, Income tax, Net wages, Pension, Trade union, Wages control, Wages expense.

41 RHYME TIME

Rhyme Time pays its employees by cheque every month and maintains a wages control account. A summary of last month's payroll transactions is shown below:

Item	£
Gross wages	10,130
Employers' NI	1,185
Employees' NI	1,006
Income tax	2,835
Employers' pension contributions	600
Employees' pension contributions	550

Record the journal entries needed in the general ledger to:

(i) Record the wages expense

(ii) Record the HMRC liability

(iii) Record the net wages paid to the employees

(iv) Record the pension liability.

(i)

Account name	Amount £	Debit ✓	Credit ✓

(ii)

Account name	Amount £	Debit ✓	Credit ✓

(iii)

Account name	Amount £	Debit ✓	Credit ✓

(iv)

Account name	Amount £	Debit ✓	Credit ✓

42   DOWN & OUT

Down & Out pays it employees by cheque every month and maintains a wages control account. A summary of last month's payroll transactions is shown below:

Item	£
Gross wages	8,542
Employers' NI	1,025
Employees' NI	940
Income tax	1,708
Trade union fees	425

Record the journal entries needed in the general ledger to:

(i)   Record the wages expense

(ii)   Record the HMRC liability

(iii)   Record the net wages paid to the employees

(iv)   Record the trade union liability.

(i)

Account name	Amount £	Debit ✓	Credit ✓

(ii)

Account name	Amount £	Debit ✓	Credit ✓

(iii)

Account name	Amount £	Debit ✓	Credit ✓

(iv)

Account name	Amount £	Debit ✓	Credit ✓

Picklist for each: Bank, Employees NI, Employers NI, HMRC, Income Tax, Net wages, Trade union, Wages control, Wages expense.

43   DEV

Dev pays its employees by cheque every month and maintains a wages control account. A summary of last month's payroll transactions is shown below:

Item	£
Gross wages	12,500
Employers' NI	1,463
Employees' NI	1,175
Income tax	3,613
Trade union fees	500

Record the journal entries needed in the general ledger to:

(i)   Record the wages expense

(ii)   Record the HMRC liability

(iii) Record the net wages paid to the employees

(iv)   Record the trade union liability.

(i)

Account name	Amount £	Debit ✓	Credit ✓

(ii)

Account name	Amount £	Debit ✓	Credit ✓

(iii)

Account name	Amount £	Debit ✓	Credit ✓

(iv)

Account name	Amount £	Debit ✓	Credit ✓

Picklist for each: Bank, Employees NI, Employers NI, HMRC, Income tax, Net wages, Pension, Trade union, Wages control, Wages expense.

44   BEDROOM BITS

A credit customer, ABC Ltd, has ceased trading, owing Bedroom Bits £2,400 including VAT.

Record the journal entries needed in the general ledger to write off the net amount and the VAT.

Account name	Amount £	Debit ✓	Credit ✓

Picklist: Irrecoverable debts, ABC Ltd, Bedroom Bits, Purchases, Payables ledger control, Sales, Receivables ledger control, VAT.

45   GARDEN GATES

A credit customer, A B Landscapes Ltd, has ceased trading, owing Garden Gates £2,600 plus VAT at 20%.

Record the journal entries needed in the general ledger to write off the net amount and the VAT.

Account name	Amount £	Debit ✓	Credit ✓

Picklist: Irrecoverable debts, A B Landscapes Ltd, Garden Gates, Purchases, Payables ledger control, Sales, Receivables ledger control, VAT.

46   CHESTNUT

On 1 December Chestnut had a balance of £46,000 on its Receivables Ledger Control Account and £31,000 on its Payables Ledger Control Account. It sold goods to Cook, one of its main suppliers, and was owed £4,000 by Cook at 1 December. Cook was owed £12,000 for goods it had sold to Chestnut.

Perform a contra and balance off the ledger accounts below. Dates are not required.

RLCA

Details	Amount £	Details	Amount £

PLCA

Details	Amount £	Details	Amount £

47 ADELA

On 1 December Adela had a balance of £49,000 on its PLCA and £56,000 on its RLCA. It purchased goods from Dulieu, one of its main customers, and owed Dulieu £11,000 at 1 December. Dulieu owed Adela £23,000 for goods it had purchased from Adela.

Perform a contra and balance off the ledger accounts below. Dates are not required.

RLCA

Details	Amount £	Details	Amount £

PLCA

Details	Amount £	Details	Amount £

48 **GANZ**

This is a customer's account in the receivables ledger.

Ganz Co

Details	Amount £	Details	Amount £
Balance b/f	4,530	Payment received	2,100
Invoice SD4564	3,210	Credit note	420

The customer has now ceased trading.

Record the journal entries needed to write off the receivable in the general ledger including VAT.

Account name	Amount £	Debit ✓	Credit ✓

Picklist: Irrecoverable debts, Beanz Co, Purchases, Payables ledger control, Sales, Receivables ledger control, VAT.

49 **ERROR TYPES 1**

Show which of the errors below are, or are not, disclosed by the trial balance.

Error in the general ledger	Error disclosed by the trial balance ✓	Error NOT disclosed by the trial balance ✓
Incorrectly calculating the balance on the Motor Vehicles account.		
Recording a receipt for commission received in the bank interest received account.		
Recording a bank receipt for bank interest received on the debit side of both the bank account and the bank interest received account.		
Recording supplier invoices on the debit side of the payables ledger control account and the credit side of the purchases account		
Recording a payment by cheque to a payable in the payables ledger control account only.		
Recording a bank payment of £124 for insurance as £142 in the insurance account and £124 in the bank account.		

50 ERROR TYPES 2

Show which of the errors below would cause an imbalance in the trial balance.

Error in the general ledger	Would cause imbalance ✓	Would NOT cause imbalance ✓
Recording a bank receipt for rent received on the credit side of both the bank account and rent received account.		
Recording a payment for new machinery in the equipment hire account.		
Recording a purchase return on the credit side of the payables ledger control account and the debit side of the purchase returns account.		
Incorrectly calculating the balance on the bank interest received account.		
Recording a payment by cheque to a payable in the bank account only.		
Recording a bank payment of £120 for stationery as £210 in both accounts.		

51 ERROR TYPES 3

Match each error description with the correct type of error by placing the appropriate answer in the table below.

Error in the general ledger	Type of error
Recording a bank receipt for rent received on the credit side of both the bank account and rent received account.	
Recording a payment for new machinery in the equipment hire account.	
Recording a purchase return on the credit side of the PLCA and the debit side of the purchase returns account.	

Picklist: Transposition error, compensating error, error of original entry, error of omission, error of commission, error of principle, reversal of entries, casting error, single entry, extraction error, two entries on one side

52   ERROR TYPES 4

Match each error description with the correct type of error by placing the appropriate answer in the table below.

Error in the general ledger	Type of error
Recording a payment to a payable in the bank account only.	
Recording a bank payment of £100 for stationery as £210 in both accounts.	
Recording a receipt for commission received in the bank interest received account.	

Picklist for all above: Transposition error, compensating error, error of original entry, error of omission, error of commission, error of principle, reversal of entries, casting error, single entry, extraction error, two entries on one side

53   ERROR TYPES 5

Match each error description with the correct type of error by placing the appropriate answer in the table below.

Error in the general ledger	Type of error
A credit sale made at the month end was not recorded.	
Recording a bank payment of £120 for stationery as £210 in the stationery account and correctly in the bank account.	
Recording a receipt for commission received in the PLCA.	

Picklist for all above: Transposition error, compensating error, error of original entry, error of omission, error of commission, error of principle, reversal of entries, casting error, single entry, extraction error, two entries on one side.

54   ERROR TYPES 6

Show which of the errors below would cause an imbalance in the trial balance.

Error in the general ledger	Would cause imbalance ✓
Forgetting to post a journal to record a contra.	
Posting the VAT on a sale transaction as a debit rather than a credit.	
Recording a cash purchase in purchases and VAT only.	
Recording the electricity expense as a debit to wages expenses, with the corresponding entry correctly credited to cash.	

55   PRINCIPLES

(a)   **Show which error is an error of principle.**

Error in the general ledger	✓
Incorrectly totalling up the sales day book.	
Recording a bank payment for rent on the debit side of the office equipment account.	
Recording rent received as a debit entry in the rent and rates account.	
Recording a payment to a supplier in the payables ledger only.	

(b)   **Show which error represents two entries on one side.**

Error in the general ledger	✓
Incorrectly totalling up the sales day book.	
Recording a bank payment for rent on the debit side of the office equipment account.	
Recording rent received as a debit entry in the rent and rates account.	
Recording a payment to a supplier in the payables ledger only.	

56   EXTRACTION

(a)   **Show which error is an error of extraction.**

Error in the general ledger	✓
Incorrectly totalling up the sales day book.	
Totalling the sales day book correctly but entering the total into the RLCA as a credit balance.	
Recording drawings as a debit to drawings and a credit to cash.	
Forgetting to post the entries for payroll.	

(b)   **Show which error represents an error of original entry.**

Error in the general ledger	✓
Posting a £210 invoice for electricity as £210 in the electricity account but £120 in the bank account.	
Posting an invoice for electricity as a debit in both the electricity and bank accounts.	
Posting electricity expense as a credit to electricity and a debit to the bank account.	
Posting a £200 invoice for electricity as £210 in both the electricity and bank account.	

57 BANK ERROR

An entry to record a bank payment of £750 for repairs has been reversed.

Record the journal entries needed in the general ledger to

(i) **remove the incorrect entry**

(ii) **record the correct entry.**

(i)

Account name	Amount £	Debit ✓	Credit ✓

(ii)

Account name	Amount £	Debit ✓	Credit ✓

Picklist for all above: Bank, Cash, Rent, Purchases, Payables ledger control, Repairs, Sales, Receivables ledger control, Suspense, VAT.

58 RENT ERROR

An entry to record a bank receipt of £500 for rent received has been reversed.

Record the journal entries needed in the general ledger to:

(i) **remove the incorrect entry**

(ii) **record the correct entry.**

(i)

Account name	Amount £	Debit ✓	Credit ✓

(ii)

Account name	Amount £	Debit ✓	Credit ✓

Picklist for all above: Bank, Cash, Rent Received, Purchases, Payables ledger control, Sales, Receivables ledger control, Suspense, VAT.

59 GAS ERROR

An entry to record a gas expense of £300 was made correctly in the bank but was posted to electricity expenses instead of gas expenses.

Record the journal entries needed in the general ledger to record the correction.

Account name	Amount £	Debit ✓	Credit ✓

60 BUILDING ERROR

An entity purchased a new building for £400,000. This amount was debited to the buildings account, but £40,000 was credited to the bank account, requiring the creation of a suspense account.

Record the journal entries needed in the general ledger to record the correction.

Account name	Amount £	Debit ✓	Credit ✓

61 SALES ERROR

A credit sale of £12,000 including VAT at 20% has been made. The full £12,000 has been debited to the RLCA and credited to sales.

Record the journal entries needed in the general ledger to record the correction.

Account name	Amount £	Debit ✓	Credit ✓

62 MOTOR ERROR

An entity incurred costs of £700 to repair a motor vehicle, which it has debited to the motor vehicles account.

Record the journal entries needed in the general ledger to record the correction.

Account name	Amount £	Debit ✓	Credit ✓

63 INVENTORY ERROR

An entity purchased goods for £720 including VAT at 20%, but recorded the purchase as £270 including VAT in the purchase day book.

Record the journal entries needed in the general ledger to record the correction.

Account name	Amount £	Debit ✓	Credit ✓

64 SUBSCRIPTIONS ERROR

A junior member of the accounts team has processed the monthly bank payment of £80 for subscriptions by debiting the bank account and crediting the subscriptions account.

Record the journal entries needed in the general ledger to record the correction.

Account name	Amount £	Debit ✓	Credit ✓

65 PURCHASE ERROR

A credit purchase of £9,000 including VAT at 20% has been made. The full £9,000 has been debited to purchases and credited to the payables ledger control account.

Record the journal entries needed in the general ledger to record the correction.

Account name	Amount £	Debit ✓	Credit ✓

66 INSURANCE ERROR

A payment for insurance of £2,700 has been made. The correct amount has been debited to the insurance expense account and credited to the payables ledger control account.

Record the journal entries needed in the general ledger to record the correction.

Account name	Amount £	Debit ✓	Credit ✓

67   CB INTERIORS

CB Interiors' initial trial balance includes a suspense account with a balance of £8,640.

The error has been traced to the purchase day-book shown below.

Purchase day-book

Date	Details	Invoice number	Total £	VAT £	Net £
30 Jun	Able Paints Ltd	2763	2,400	400	2,000
30 Jun	Matley Materials	2764	3,120	520	2,600
30 Jun	Teesdale Parts	2765	4,080	680	3,400
	Totals		960	1,600	8,000

Identify the error and record the journal entries needed in the general ledger to

(i)   remove the incorrect entry

(ii)   record the correct entry

(iii)   remove the suspense account balance.

(i)

Account name	Amount £	Debit ✓	Credit ✓

(ii)

Account name	Amount £	Debit ✓	Credit ✓

(iii)

Account name	Amount £	Debit ✓	Credit ✓

Picklist for all above: Able Paints Ltd, Matley Materials, Teesdale Parts, Purchases, Purchases day-book, Payables ledger control, Purchases returns, Purchases returns day-book, Sales, Sales day-book, Receivables ledger control, Sales returns, Sales returns day-book, Suspense, VAT.

68 ROGER DODGER

Roger Dodger's initial trial balance includes a suspense account with a balance of £360.

The error has been traced to the purchase returns day-book shown below.

Purchase returns day-book

DATE 20XX	Details	Note number	Total £	VAT £	Net £
30 Jun	Dennis Designs Ltd	421	1,200	200	1,000
30 Jun	XYZ Ltd	422	1,920	320	1,600
30 Jun	Denby Prints	423	4,800	800	4,000
	Totals		7,920	1,680	6,600

Identify the error and record the journal entries needed in the general ledger to:

(i)   remove the incorrect entry

(ii) record the correct entry

(iii) remove the suspense account balance.

(i)

Account name	Amount £	Debit ✓	Credit ✓

(ii)

Account name	Amount £	Debit ✓	Credit ✓

(iii)

Account name	Amount £	Debit ✓	Credit ✓

Picklist for all above: Dennis Designs Ltd, XYZ Ltd, Denby Prints, Purchases, Purchases day-book, Payables ledger control, Purchases returns, Purchases returns day-book, Sales, Sales day-book, Receivables ledger control, Sales returns, Sales returns day-book, Suspense, VAT.

69   A CUT ABOVE

A Cut Above's initial trial balance includes a suspense account with a balance of £230.

The error has been traced to the purchase returns day-book shown below.

Purchases returns day-book

Date 20XX	Details	Returns note number	Total £	VAT £	Net £
30 April	A & S Timber Ltd	12 – 356K	576	96	480
30 April	GB Tools	AB768 – 2	816	136	680
30 April	LAH Ltd	236	4,560	760	3,800
	Totals		6,182	992	4,960

Identify the error and record the journal entries needed in the general ledger to:

(i)   remove the incorrect entry

(ii)   record the correct entry

(iii) remove the suspense account balance.

(i)

Account name	Amount £	Debit ✓	Credit ✓

(ii)

Account name	Amount £	Debit ✓	Credit ✓

(iii)

Account name	Amount £	Debit ✓	Credit ✓

Picklist for all above: A & S Timber Ltd, GB Tools, LAH Ltd, Purchases, Purchases day-book, Payables ledger control, Purchases returns, Purchase returns day-books, Sales, Sales day-book, Receivables ledger control, Sales returns, Sales returns day-books, Suspense, VAT.

70   RESTCO

Restco's initial trial balance includes a suspense account with a balance of £720.

The error has been traced to the sales day-book shown below.

Sales day-book

Date 20XX	Details	Invoice number	Total £	VAT £	Net £
30 Jun	Ben's Build Ltd	11232	2,160	360	1,800
30 Jun	OPP Ltd	11233	3,360	560	2,800
30 Jun	Outside Capers	11234	5,040	840	4,200
	Totals		10,560	1,760	8,080

Identify the error and record the journal entries needed in the general ledger to

(i)   remove the incorrect entry

(ii)   record the correct entry

(iii)   remove the suspense account balance.

(i)

Account name	Amount £	Debit ✓	Credit ✓

(ii)

Account name	Amount £	Debit ✓	Credit ✓

(iii)

Account name	Amount £	Debit ✓	Credit ✓

Picklist for all above: Ben's Build Ltd, OPP Ltd, Outside Capers, Purchases, Purchases day-book, Payables ledger control, Purchases returns, Purchases returns day-book,   Sales, Sales day-book, Receivables ledger control, Sales returns, Sales returns day-book, Suspense, VAT.

71   JOHNNY JOINER

Johnny Joiner's trial balance was extracted and did not balance. The debit column of the trial balance totalled £442,735 and the credit column totalled £428,372.

(a)   **What entry would be made in the suspense account to balance the trial balance?**

Account name	Amount £	Debit ✓	Credit ✓
Suspense			

(b)   The error has been traced to sales, which were posted as £241,874 instead of £256,237.

Record the journal entries needed in the general ledger to record the correction.

Account name	Amount £	Debit ✓	Credit ✓

72   BUCKLEY DRAINS

Buckley Drains' trial balance was extracted and did not balance. The debit column of the trial balance totalled £336,728 and the credit column totalled £325,923.

(a)   **What entry would be made in the suspense account to balance the trial balance?**

Account name	Amount £	Debit ✓	Credit ✓
Suspense			

(b)   The error has been traced to an unpaid invoice for advertising, which was recorded correctly in advertising expenses but nowhere else.

Record the journal entries needed in the general ledger to record the correction.

Account name	Amount £	Debit ✓	Credit ✓

(c)   **Show one reason for maintaining the journal**

	✓
To correct errors only	
To correct errors and record transactions that have not been recorded in any other book of prime entry	
To record transactions from every other book of prime entry.	

73 MENDONCA

Mendonca's trial balance was extracted and did not balance. The debit column of the trial balance totalled £643,475 and the credit column totalled £641,495

(a) **What entry would be made in the suspense account to balance the trial balance?**

Account name	Amount £	Debit ✓	Credit ✓

(b) The error has been traced to the posting of the wages payment. The total payment made was £3,200. This was incorrectly made in both the wages and bank account. The amount recorded in wages was £2,300, with a credit made to the bank of £320.

Record the journal entries needed in the general ledger to record the correction.

Account name	Amount £	Debit ✓	Credit ✓

74 BEASANT

Beasant's trial balance was extracted and did not balance. The debit column of the trial balance totalled £630,000 and the credit column totalled £615,000.

(a) **What entry would be made in the suspense account to balance the trial balance?**

Account name	Amount £	Debit ✓	Credit ✓
Suspense			

(b) The error has been traced to a late credit sale. The full amount of the sale (including VAT at 20%) was correctly recorded in the RLCA but no other entries were made.

Record the journal entries needed in the general ledger to record the correction.

Account name	Amount £	Debit ✓	Credit ✓

(c) **Show one reason for maintaining the journal**

	✓
To detect fraud	
To record non-regular transactions	
To record goods sold on credit	

75   PAT'S CAFE

Pat's Cafe's trial balance did not balance. The debit column totalled £67,410 and the credit column totalled £72,060.

(a)   What entry would be made in the suspense account to balance the trial balance?

Account name	Amount £	Debit ✓	Credit ✓

The journal entries to correct the bookkeeping errors, and a list of balances as they appear in the trial balance, are shown below.

Journal entries

Account name	Debit £	Credit £
Bank interest paid	114	
Bank interest received		114
Insurance	150	
Suspense		150
Motor vehicles	4,500	
Suspense		4,500

Account name

Account name	Debit £	Credit £
Bank interest paid	121	
Bank interest received	53	
Insurance	400	
Motor vehicles	2,000	

(b)   Complete the table below to show the new balances, and whether each will be a debit or a credit.

Account name	Balance £	Debit ✓	Credit ✓
Bank interest paid			
Bank interest received			
Insurance			
Motor vehicles			

76   TWINKLE'S TRINKETS

Twinkle's Trinkets trial balance did not balance. The debit column totalled £112,340 and the credit column totalled £111,564.

(a)   What entry would be made in the suspense account to balance the trial balance?

Account name	Amount £	Debit ✓	Credit ✓
Suspense			

The journal entries to correct the bookkeeping errors, and a list of balances as they appear in the trial balance, are shown below.

Journal entries

Account name	Debit £	Credit £
Motor expenses	324	
Suspense		324
Suspense	1,100	
Repairs and renewals		1,100
Rent payable	500	
Rent received		500

Account name

Account name	Debit £	Credit £
Motor expenses	8,420	
Repairs and renewals	2,310	
Rent payable	3,200	
Rent received		1,200

(b)   Complete the table below to show the new balances, and whether each will be a debit or a credit.

Account name	Balance £	Debit ✓	Credit ✓
Motor expenses			
Repairs and renewals			
Rent payable			
Rent received			

77   SPARKS AND MENCER

Sparks and Mencer's trial balance included a suspense account. All the bookkeeping errors have now been traced and the journal entries shown below have been recorded.

The journal entries to correct the bookkeeping errors, and a list of balances as they appear in the trial balance, are shown below.

Journal entries

Account name	Debit £	Credit £
Heat and light		545
Suspense	545	
Rates	786	
Suspense		786
Loan interest expense	269	
Rent received		269

Account name

Account name	Debit £	Credit £
Heat and light	1,200	
Rates	630	
Loan interest expense		104
Rent received	150	

Complete the table below to show the new balances, and whether each will be a debit or a credit.

Account name	Balance £	Debit ✔	Credit ✔
Heat and light			
Rates			
Loan interest expense			
Rent received			

PRODUCE THE TRIAL BALANCE

78 RAVI'S RACERS

On 30 June Ravi's Racers extracted an initial trial balance which did not balance, and a suspense account was opened. On 1 July journal entries were prepared to correct the errors that had been found, and clear the suspense account. The list of balances in the initial trial balance, and the journal entries to correct the errors, are shown below.

Re-draft the trial balance by placing the figures in the debit or credit column. You should take into account the journal entries which will clear the suspense account.

	Original balances extracted on 30 June £	New balance following adjustment on 1 July £	Debit ✓	Credit ✓
Motor vehicles	24,200			
Plant and equipment	22,350			
Inventory	9,000			
Cash at bank	11,217			
Cash	150			
Receivables ledger control	131,275			
Payables ledger control	75,336			
VAT owing to HMRC	15,127			
Capital	14,417			
Bank loan	12,500			
Sales	276,132			
Purchases	152,476			
Wages	35,465			
Motor expenses	3,617			
Repairs and renewals	2,103			
Rent and rates	3,283			
Light and heat	4,012			
Insurance	4,874			
Sundry expenses	1,230			
Suspense account (credit balance)	11,740			

Journal entries

Account name	Debit £	Credit £
Capital		9,500
Suspense	9,500	
Capital		2,330
Suspense	2,330	

Account name	Debit £	Credit £
Suspense	1,230	
Sundry expenses		1,230
Sundry expenses	1,320	
Suspense		1,320

79 PERCY POTS

On 30 June Percy Pots extracted an initial trial balance which did not balance, and a suspense account was opened. On 1 July journal entries were prepared to correct the errors that had been found, and clear the suspense account. The list of balances in the initial trial balance, and the journal entries to correct the errors, are shown below.

Re-draft the trial balance by placing the figures in the debit or credit column. You should take into account the journal entries which will clear the suspense account.

	Balances extracted on 30 June £	Balances at 1 July	
		Debit £	Credit £
Motor vehicles	22,348		
Fixtures and fittings	9,234		
Inventory	4,800		
Bank	2,661		
Petty cash	100		
Receivables ledger control	61,025		
Payables ledger control	35,275		
VAT owing to HMRC	4,630		
Capital	4,852		
Sales	142,378		
Sales returns	1,780		
Purchases	69,276		
Wages	13,500		
Motor expenses	873		
Office expenses	1,796		
Rent and rates	1,276		
Heat and light	1,022		
Insurance	1,629		
Miscellaneous expenses	1,047		
Suspense account (credit balance)	5,232		
Totals			

Journal entries

Account name	Debit £	Credit £
Bank		2,661
Suspense	2,661	
Bank		2,661
Suspense	2,661	

Account name	Debit £	Credit £
Sales returns	1,870	
Suspense		1,870
Sales returns		1,780
Suspense	1,780	

80   IVOR ISLAND

On 30 April Ivor Island extracted an initial trial balance which did not balance, and a suspense account was opened. On 1 May journal entries were prepared to correct the errors that had been found, and clear the suspense account. The list of balances in the initial trial balance, and the journal entries to correct the errors, are shown below.

Redraft the trial balance by placing the figures in the debit or credit column. You should take into account the journal entries below which will clear the suspense account.

	Balances extracted on 30 April	Balances at 1 May	
		Debit £	Credit £
Motor vehicles	8,454		
Office building	28,676		
Inventory	15,369		
Bank	26,984		
Petty cash	459		
Receivables ledger control	35,987		
Payables ledger control	26,942		
VAT (owing from HMRC)	231		
Capital	98,106		
Sales	96,325		
Purchase returns (credit balance)	3,654		
Purchases	68,975		
Wages	18,564		
Motor expenses	1,269		
Office expenses	5,798		
Rates	4,300		
Heat and light	5,423		
Insurance	3,365		
Miscellaneous expenses	2,645		
Suspense account (credit balance)	1,472		

Journal entries:

Account name	Debit £	Credit £
VAT		586
Suspense	586	
VAT		586
Suspense	586	

Account name	Debit £	Credit £
Purchase returns		2,556
Suspense	2,556	
Purchase returns	2,256	
Suspense		2,256

81 RING OF ROSES

On 30 June Ring of Roses extracted an initial trial balance which did not balance, and a suspense account was opened. On 1 July journal entries were prepared to correct the errors that had been found, and clear the suspense account. The list of balances in the initial trial balance, and the journal entries to correct the errors, are shown below.

Re-draft the trial balance by placing the figures in the debit or credit column. You should take into account the journal entries which will clear the suspense account.

	Balances extracted on 30 June £	Balances at 1 July	
		Debit £	Credit £
Motor vehicles	27,625		
Plant and equipment	5,000		
Inventory	7,350		
Cash at bank	7,195		
Cash	200		
Receivables ledger control	121,275		
Payables ledger control	67,323		
VAT owing to HMRC	10,098		
Capital	22,291		
Sales	253,727		
Sales returns	2,123		
Purchases	128,476		
Purchase returns	9,872		
Wages	34,250		
Motor expenses	1,797		
Office expenses	4,946		
Rent and rates	2,321		
Heat and light	3,123		
Insurance	4,205		
Suspense account (debit balance)	13,425		
Totals			

Journal entries

Account name	Debit £	Credit £
Bank	7,150	
Suspense		7,150
Purchases	6,455	
Suspense		6,455
Suspense	4,205	
Insurance		4,205
Insurance	4,025	
Suspense		4,025

82   HEARN

On 30 June Hearn extracted an initial trial balance which did not balance, and a suspense account was opened. On 1 July the following errors were noted:

1   A rent payment of £430 had been correctly included in the bank, but included within rent expenses as £340.

2   An irrecoverable debt of £600 plus VAT at 20% had been credited correctly to the RLCA, but the only debit entry was £600 to irrecoverable debts.

Complete the journal to correct the errors, and re-draft the trial balance by placing figures into the debit or credit column. Your re-drafted trial balance should take into account the journal entries you have made.

Journal entries

Account name	Debit £	Credit £

	Balances extracted on 30 June £	Balances at 1 July	
		Debit £	Credit £
Receivables ledger control	34,560		
Payables ledger control	21,420		
VAT owing to HMRC	3,412		
Capital	50,000		
Sales	201,327		
Sales returns	1,465		
Purchases	87,521		
Purchase returns	252		
Plant and equipment	15,200		
Motor expenses	4,310		
Office expenses	10,321		
Rent and rates	21,420		
Heat and light	8,920		
Wages	53,205		
Irrecoverable debt	1,450		
Office equipment	42,030		
Bank overdraft	4201		
Suspense account (debit balance)	210		
Totals			

83 RODMAN

On 30 June, Rodman extracted an initial trial balance, which did not balance, and a suspense account was opened. On 1 July, the following errors were noted:

1 A VAT refund of £1,250 received from HMRC was recorded in the bank, but no other entry was made.

2 A wages payment of £4,300 was credited to both the bank and wages.

Complete the journal to correct the errors, and re-draft the trial balance by placing figures into the debit or credit column. Your re-drafted trial balance should take into account the journal entries you have made.

Journal entries

Account name	Debit £	Credit £

	Balances extracted on 30 June £	Balances at 1 July	
		Debit £	Credit £
Receivables ledger control	38,070		
Payables ledger control	20,310		
VAT owed from HMRC	2,510		
Capital	70,000		
Sales	153,488		
Sales returns	2,135		
Purchases	63,261		
Purchase returns	542		
Plant and equipment	17,319		
Motor expenses	3,214		
Office expenses	6,421		
Rent and rates	17,414		
Heat and light	6,421		
Wages	45,532		
Irrecoverable debt	1,532		
Office equipment	35,313		
Bank overdraft	2,152		
Suspense account (debit balance)	7,350		
	Totals		

84   SMITH & SON

Below is a list of balances to be transferred to the trial balance of Smith & Son at 31 Dec.

Place the figures in the debit or credit column, as appropriate, and total each column.

Account name	Amount £	Debit £	Credit £
Fixtures and fittings	8,250		
Capital	18,400		
Bank overdraft	4,870		
Petty cash control	350		
Receivables ledger control (RLCA)	42,870		
Payables ledger control (PLCA)	23,865		
VAT owed to tax authorities	10,245		
Inventory	9,870		
Loan from bank	22,484		
Sales	180,264		
Sales returns	5,420		
Purchases	129,030		
Purchases returns	2,678		
Discount allowed	2,222		
Discount received	3,432		
Heat and Light	1,490		
Motor expenses	2,354		
Wages	42,709		
Rent and rates	10,600		
Repairs	3,020		
Hotel expenses	1,890		
Telephone	2,220		
Delivery costs	1,276		
Miscellaneous expenses	2,667		
Totals			

85   EXPIALIDOCIOUS LTD

Below is a list of balances to be transferred to the trial balance of Expialidocious Ltd as at 31 July.

Place the figures in the debit or credit column, as appropriate, and total each column.

Account name	Amount £	Debit £	Credit £
Capital	25,360		
Petty cash control	250		
Loan from bank	11,600		
Receivables ledger control (RLCA)	159,242		
Payables ledger control (PLCA)	83,682		
Motor vehicles	35,900		
Inventory	28,460		
Bank overdraft	10,063		
VAT owed from tax authorities	15,980		
Purchases	343,014		
Purchases returns	1,515		
Wages	56,150		
Motor expenses	2,950		
Interest income	400		
Sales	532,900		
Sales returns	5,760		
Stationery	1,900		
Light & heat	6,500		
Discount received	200		
Discount allowed	2,160		
Interest paid on overdraft	550		
Travel	1,800		
Marketing	650		
Telephone	1,510		
Miscellaneous expenses	2,944		
Totals			

86   DIXON FURNITURE

Below is a list of balances to be transferred to the trial balance of Dixon Furniture as at 31 Jan.

Place the figures in the debit or credit column, as appropriate, and total each column.

Account name	Amount £	Debit £	Credit £
Motor vehicles	40,100		
Capital	35,000		
Petty cash control	150		
Bank balance	14,654		
Wages	37,890		
Travel expenses	1,500		
Rental income	1,000		
Sales	435,600		
Loan from bank	10,000		
Receivables ledger control (RLCA)	127,456		
Inventory	22,500		
Payables ledger control (PLCA)	91,250		
VAT due to tax authorities	12,500		
Purchases	325,600		
Sales returns	6,500		
Purchases returns	1,250		
Sundry expenses	3,600		
Electricity expense	450		
Bank interest received	360		
Fuel expense	900		
Discount received	600		
Discount allowed	1,560		
Advertising	300		
Telephone	1,900		
Miscellaneous expenses	2,500		
Totals			

87   ARCHIE

Below are the balances of the debit and credit columns of Archie's partially prepared trial balance. As the trial balance is not yet complete it does not balance.

Debit £	Credit £
31,150	
	87,000
4,050	
58,920	
	1,700
11,075	
	23,111
6,250	
3,990	

(a)   **Calculate the total of each of the debit and credit columns of the partially complete trial balance.**

Debit £	Credit £

There are now three final balances to be transferred to the trial balance.

Account name	Balance £
Drawings	2,350
Payables ledger control	6,859
Discounts allowed	885

(b)   **Transfer each balance to the debit or credit column of the trial balance extract below.**

Account name	Debit £	Credit £
Drawings		
Payables ledger control		
Discounts allowed		

The trial balance should now balance.

(c)   **Calculate the final total to be entered into the debit and credit columns of the trial balance.**

£

The trial balance for a different organisation is being prepared.

These are the balances available so far:

Receivables ledger accounts	Balance £
Original Ltd	8,900
Evie & Joe	10,880

Payables ledger accounts	Balance £
Jacob & Danny	1,280
PPR LLP	6,122

General ledger accounts	Balance £
Fixtures and Fittings	29,000
Capital	60,500
Discounts allowed	1,035
Rent received	13,670
Bank (in funds)	12,600
Sales	145,000

(d) Identify SIX accounts that will appear in the trial balance and whether they will be transferred to the debit or credit column.

Account name	Debit ✓	Credit ✓	Does not appear in the trial balance ✓
Fixtures and fittings			
Capital			
Discounts allowed			
Rent received			
Bank			
Sales			
Original Ltd			
Evie & Joe			
Jacob & Danny			
PPR LLP			

88 HARRISON

Below are the balances of the debit and credit columns of Harrison's partially prepared trial balance. As the trial balance is not yet complete it does not balance.

Debit £	Credit £
28,230	
	95,000
670	
61,000	
	835
9,423	
	17,555
5,800	
4,032	

(a) **Calculate the total of each of the debit and credit columns of the partially complete trial balance.**

Debit £	Credit £

There are now three final balances to be transferred to the trial balance.

Account name	Balance £
Drawings	8,000
Capital	3,315
Discounts received	450

(b) **Transfer each balance to the debit or credit column of the trial balance extract below.**

Account name	Debit £	Credit £
Drawings		
Capital		
Discounts received		

The trial balance should now balance.

(c) **Calculate the final total to be entered into the debit and credit columns of the trial balance.**

£

The trial balance for a different organisation is being prepared.

These are the balances available so far:

Receivables ledger accounts	Balance £
Dave & Malc Co	3,120
Amy & Molly	4,500

Payables ledger accounts	Balance £
Peter & Paul	8,000
Morris Ltd	4,500

General ledger accounts	Balance £
Motor vehicles	22,550
Capital	45,000
Discounts received	450
Interest paid	660
Bank overdraft	6,700
Purchases	6,000

(d)   Identify SIX accounts that will appear in the trial balance and whether they will be transferred to the debit or credit column

Account name	Debit ✓	Credit ✓	Does not appear in the trial balance ✓
Motor vehicles			
Capital			
Discounts received			
Interest paid			
Bank overdraft			
Purchases			
Dave & Malc Co			
Amy & Molly			
Peter & Paul			
Morris Ltd			

89   KOOKABURRA

Below is an extract of balances from Kookaburra's trial balance.

(a)   Calculate and insert the total of each of the debit and credit columns of the partially prepared trial balance.

Account name	Debit £	Credit £
Plant and equipment	106,340	
Receivables ledger control (RLCA)	36,470	
Bank	12,590	
Inventory	18,240	
Payables ledger control (PLCA)		27,021
Capital		50,000
Bank loan		2,590
Sales		625,640
Purchases	295,100	
Wages	32,410	
Administrative expenses	1,280	
Rent and rates	12,490	
Heat and light	4,291	
Entertainment expenses	456	
Telephone and broadband expenses	3,214	
Totals		

Shown below are the three final balances to be transferred to the trial balance.

(b)   Transfer each balance to the debit or credit column of the trial balance extract below.

Account name	Amount £	Debit £	Credit £
Purchases returns	14,980		
Land and Buildings	197,000		
Petty cash	350		

The trial balance should now balance meaning the totals of the debit and credit columns should agree.

(c)   Calculate the final total entered into the debit and credit columns of the trial balance.

£

The trial balance for a different organisation is being prepared and balances have been provided from the accounting records.

(d) **You are required to identify whether these accounts appear in the trial balance and if so whether they would be transferred to the debit or credit column.**

Receivables ledger

Account name	Account balance	Transfers to the trial balance in the DEBIT column ✓	Transfers to the trial balance in the CREDIT column ✓	Does not transfer to the trial balance ✓
Riley Racing	£3,250			
Kat's Cakes	£2,560			

Payables ledger

Account name	Account balance	Transfers to the trial balance in the DEBIT column ✓	Transfers to the trial balance in the CREDIT column ✓	Does not transfer to the trial balance ✓
VK Supplies	£2,364			
TAF Ltd	£7,171			

General ledger

Account name	Account balance	Transfers to the trial balance in the DEBIT column ✓	Transfers to the trial balance in the CREDIT column ✓	Does not transfer to the trial balance ✓
Sales returns	£23,910			
Bank overdraft	£2,185			

90   ALAN

The following are the year end balances in Alan's general ledger:

	£
Sales	628,000
Cost of sales	458,000
General expenses	138,000
Payables ledger control	54,000
Receivables ledger control	?
Bank (in funds)	61,000
Capital	86,000

(a)   **If Alan's trial balance balances, what is the missing figure for the receivables ledger control?**

   A   £61,000

   B   £111,000

   C   £233,000

   D   £387,000

(b)   **Taking into consideration the answer to part (a) what is the trial balance total?**

   £ [   ]

(c)   **Which of the following balances would appear on the same side in the trial balance?**

   A   Drawings and bank loan

   B   Drawings and purchases

   C   Capital and purchases

   D   Capital and rental expense

Section 2

ANSWERS TO PRACTICE QUESTIONS

USE CONTROL ACCOUNTS

1   MONSTER MUNCHIES

(a)

Details	Amount £	Debit ✓	Credit ✓
Balance of receivables at 1 June	48,000	✓	
Goods sold on credit	12,415	✓	
Receipts from credit customers	22,513		✓
Discount allowed	465		✓
Sales returns from credit customers	320		✓

(b)

Dr £37,117	✓

(c)

	£
Receivables ledger control account balance as at 30 June	37,117
Total of subsidiary (receivables) ledger accounts as at 30 June	36,797
Difference	320

(d)

Sales returns may have been omitted from the subsidiary ledger.	
Discounts allowed may have been omitted from the subsidiary ledger.	
Sales returns may have been entered in the subsidiary ledger twice.	✓
Discounts allowed may have been entered in the subsidiary ledger twice.	✓

(e)

Reconciliation of the receivables ledger control account assures managers that the amount showing as owed to suppliers is correct.	
Reconciliation of the receivables ledger control account assures managers that the amount showing as outstanding from customers is correct.	✓
Reconciliation of the receivables ledger control account will show if a purchase invoice has been omitted from the payables ledger.	
Reconciliation of the receivables ledger control account will show if a purchase invoice has been omitted from the receivables ledger.	

2   JACK'S BOX

(a)

Details	Amount £	Debit ✓	Credit ✓
Balance of receivables at 1 April	60,589	✓	
Goods sold on credit	26,869	✓	
Payments received from credit customers	29,411		✓
Discount allowed	598		✓
Goods returned from credit customers	1,223		✓

(b)

Dr £55,030	
Cr £55,030	
Dr £56,226	✓
Cr £56,226	
Dr £52,584	
Cr £52,584	

(c)

	£
Receivables Ledger control account balances as at 30 April	56,226
Total of subsidiary (receivables) ledger accounts as at 30 April	55,003
Difference	1,223

(d)

	✓
Sales returns may have been omitted from the subsidiary ledger.	
Discounts allowed may have been omitted from the subsidiary ledger.	
Sales returns have been entered into the subsidiary ledger twice.	✓
Discounts allowed have been entered into subsidiary ledger twice.	

(e)

	✓
Reconciliation of the receivables ledger control account will show if a purchase invoice has been omitted from the payables ledger.	
Reconciliation of the receivables ledger control account will show if a sales invoice has been omitted from the payables ledger.	.
Reconciliation of the receivables ledger control account assures managers that the amount showing due to suppliers is correct.	
Reconciliation of the receivables ledger control account assures managers that the amount showing due from customers is correct.	✓

3   CILLA'S SINKS

(a)

Details	Amount £	Debit ✓	Credit ✓
Balance of payables at 1 June	52,150		✓
Goods bought on credit	19,215		✓
Payments made to credit suppliers	19,073	✓	
Discount received	284	✓	
Goods returned to credit suppliers	1,023	✓	

(b)

Cr £50,985	✓

(c)

	£
Payables ledger control account balance as at 30 June	50,985
Total of subsidiary (payable) ledger accounts as at 30 June	52,008
Difference	1,023

(d)

Goods returned may have been omitted from the subsidiary ledger.	✓
Discounts received may have been omitted from the subsidiary ledger.	
Goods returned may have been entered in the subsidiary ledger twice.	
Discounts received may have been entered into the subsidiary ledger twice.	

(e)

Reconciliation of the PLCA will help to identify any supplier invoices that have been omitted in error.	✓
Reconciliation of the payables ledger control account will show if a sales invoice has been omitted from the payables ledger.	
Reconciliation of the payables ledger control account will show if a sales invoice has been omitted from the receivables ledger.	
Reconciliation of the payables ledger control account will help to identify any discounts allowed that have been omitted in error.	

4   VIK'S TRICKS

(a)

Details	Amount £	Debit ✓	Credit ✓
Balance of receivables at 1 June	58,120	✓	
Goods sold on credit	20,013	✓	
Receipts from credit customers	22,327		✓
Discount allowed	501		✓
Sales returns from credit customers	970		✓

(b)

Dr £54,335	✓

(c)

	£
Receivables ledger control account balance as at 30 June	54,335
Total of subsidiary (receivables) ledger accounts as at 30 June	55,305
Difference	970

(d)

Discounts allowed may have been entered in the subsidiary ledger twice.	
Discounts allowed may have been omitted from the subsidiary ledger.	✓
Sales returns may have been entered in the subsidiary ledger twice.	
Sales returns may have been omitted from the subsidiary ledger.	✓

(e)

Reconciliation of the receivables ledger control account will help to identify any customer invoices that have been omitted in error.	✓
Reconciliation of the receivables ledger control account will show if a purchase invoice has been omitted from the receivables ledger.	
Reconciliation of the receivables ledger control account will show if a purchase invoice has been omitted from the payables ledger.	
Reconciliation of the receivables ledger control account will help to identify any discounts received that have been omitted in error.	

5   ZHANG

(a)

RLCA

Details	Amount £	Details	Amount £
Balance b/d	65,830	SBD overcast	1,200
		Discount given	210
		Balance c/d	64,420
	65,830		**65,830**
Balance b/d	64,420		

List of balances:

	£
Total:	65,090
Contra missing	(800)
Credit note posted twice	130
Revised total:	64,420

(b)   Show whether the following statements are true or false:

	True ✓	False ✓
An aged trade receivables analysis is used when chasing customers for outstanding payments.	✓	
An aged trade receivables analysis is sent to credit customers when payments are being requested.		✓

6   HANDYSIDE

(a)

PLCA

Details	Amount £	Details	Amount £
Returns	120	Balance b/d	25,360
		Missing invoice	720
Balance c/d	25,960		
	26,080		**26,080**
		Balance b/d	25,960

List of balances:

	£
Total	26,000
Net amount entered	400
Returns	(350)
Transposition error	(90)
Revised total	25,960

(b)   Show whether the following statements are true or false:

	True ✓	False ✓
The payables ledger control account enables a business to see how much is owed to individual suppliers		✓
The payables ledger control account total should reconcile to the total of the list of supplier balances in the payables ledger	✓	

7 RING TELEPHONE

(a)

VAT control

Details	Amount £	Details	Amount £
Sales returns	360	Sales	30,600
Purchases	16,200	Cash sales	48
		Purchases returns	1,160
Balance c/d	15,248		
	31,808		**31,808**
		Balance b/d	15,248

(b) No – it is £15,248 owed **to** HMRC

(c)

	£	Debit	Credit
Balance brought down	38,900	✓	

Workings:

VAT control

Details	Amount £	Details	Amount £
Debit balances	93,800	Credit balances	54,400
Purchase of equipment	400	Cash sales	900
		Balance c/d	38,900
	94,200		**94,200**
Balance b/d	38,900		

8 JO'S JOINERS

(a)

VAT Control

Details	Amount £	Details	Amount £
Purchases	21,000	Sales	31,200
Sales returns	720	Cash sales	120
		Purchases returns	1,088
Balance c/d	10,688		
	32,408		**32,408**
		Balance b/d	10,688

(b) Yes

9   KOFI'S KABINS

(a)

VAT control

Details	Amount £	Details	Amount £
Sales returns	600	Sales	35,960
Purchases	20,040	Cash sales	112
		Purchases returns	1,144
Balance c/d	16,576		
	37,216		**37,216**
		Balance b/d	16,576

(b)   No – the amount owed to HMRC is £16,576.

10   DISLEY

(a)

	£	Debit	Credit
VAT total in the sales day book	65,420		65,420
VAT total in the purchases day book	21,340	21,340	
VAT total in the sales returns day book	480	480	
VAT balance brought forward, owed to HMRC	24,910		24,910
VAT on irrecoverable debts	830	830	
VAT on petty cash expenses paid	210	210	

(b)   No – the amount owed to HMRC is £67,470.

(c)

	£	Debit	Credit
Balance brought down	19,730		✓

Workings:

VAT control

Details	Amount £	Details	Amount £
Debit balances	42,300	Credit balances	61,250
Irrecoverable debt	200	Discounts received	980
Balance c/d	19,730		
	62,230		**62,230**
		Balance b/d	19,730

11   KERR

(a)   **Show whether each item is a debit or credit balance by copying the amount into the correct column**

	£	Debit	Credit
VAT total in the purchase returns day book	1,320		1,320
VAT total in discounts received day book	400		400
VAT on cash purchases	2,670	2,670	
VAT on the sale of equipment	970		970
VAT total in discounts allowed day book	500	500	
VAT refund received from HMRC	2,580		2,580
VAT on cash sales	5,880		5,880
VAT balance brought forward, due from HMRC	2,580	2,580	

(b)   Yes – the amount owed is correct

12   NILSSON

(a)

	£	Debit	Credit
VAT total in the sales day book	54,670		54,670
VAT total in the purchases day book	26,340	26,340	
VAT total in the sales returns day book	1,240	1,240	
VAT total in the purchases returns day book	760		760
VAT on sale of equipment	3,210		3,210
VAT on petty cash expenses paid	500	500	
VAT balance brought forward, owed to HMRC	42,180		42,180
VAT on irrecoverable debts	430	430	
VAT paid to HMRC during the period	32,150	32,150	
VAT on cash sales	6,540		6,540
VAT on cash purchases	7,520	7,520	
VAT total in discounts allowed day book	1,130	1,130	
VAT total in discounts received day book	980		980

(b)   Yes – the amount owed is correct

RECONCILE A BANK STATEMENT WITH THE CASH BOOK

13 BLOSSOM BLOOMS

(a)

Checks to be made	Cheque	Telephone credit card payment
Check expiry date	✓	
Check issue number	✓	✓
Check not post dated		✓
Check security number	✓	
Check words and figures match		✓
Check card has not been tampered with	✓	✓

(b)
When Blossom Blooms makes payments to suppliers by debit card, the amount paid affects the bank current account

True

When Blossom Blooms makes payments to suppliers by credit card, the amount paid affects the bank current account

False

14 PARI'S PARROTS

(a)

Checks to be made	Cheque ✓	Telephone credit card payment ✓
Check expiry date		✓
Check issue number		
Check not posted dated	✓	
Check security number		✓
Check words and figures match	✓	
Check card has not been tampered with		

(b)
When Pari's Parrots makes payments to suppliers by credit card, the amount does not leave the bank current account immediately

True

When Pari's Parrots makes payments to suppliers by debit card, the amount paid affects the bank current account

True

15 BANK EFFECTS 1

Which TWO balances will NOT reduce funds in the bank balance of the payer at the date of payment?

Standing order	
Cheque payment	✓
CHAPS payment	
Credit card payment	✓

16 BANK EFFECTS 2

Which THREE balances WILL reduce funds in the bank balance of the payer at the date of payment?

Direct debit	✓
Building society cheque payment	
Debit card payment	✓
BACS payment	✓

17 METHODS OF PAYMENT 1

Match the payment need with the most likely method of payment to be used.

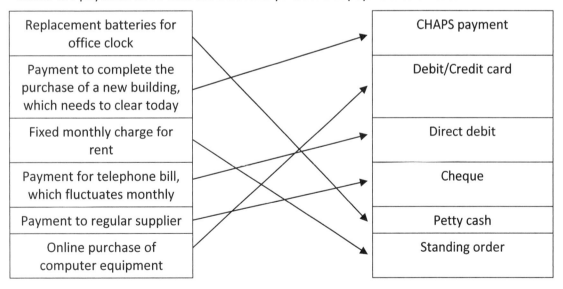

18   METHODS OF PAYMENT 2

Match the payment with the description below

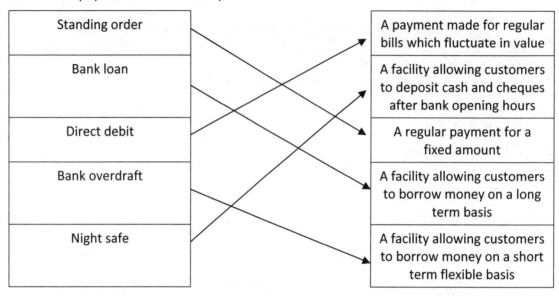

19   RIVERS LTD

(a) – (c)

Date 20XX	Details	Bank £	Date 20XX	Cheque number	Details	Bank £
01 June	Balance b/d	3,115	01 June	111013	Indigo Beds	650
17 June	Bracken Ltd	300	01 June	111014	DirectFit	1,420
21 June	Airfleet Interiors	560	01 June	111015	Langdon	60
22 June	Harris Homes	333	01 June	111016	QPF Ltd	615
12 June	Ayreshire Build	970	02 June	111017	OMD Ltd	815
23 June	Bank interest	15	02 June	111018	Hamden Ltd	450
			13 June	111019	Freeman & Cope	522
			13 June		Collins	175
			20 June		Rent	500
			23 June		Bank charges	20
			23 June		Balance c/d	66
		5,293				5,293
24 June	Balance b/d	66				

20   LUXURY BATHROOMS

(a) – (c)

Date	Details	Bank	Date	Cheque	Details	Bank
01 April	Balance b/d	17,845	01 April	120045	R Sterling Ltd	8,850
19 April	Olsen & Lane	2,150	01 April	120046	Bert Cooper	2,250
22 April	Frith Ltd	685	01 April	120047	Hetko & Sons	64
22 April	Hodgetts & Co	282	02 April	120048	Barrett Ltd	3,256
04 April	Ricketts & Co	465	02 April	120049	K Plomer	542
			08 April	120050	I&E Brown	655
			08 April	120051	T Roberts	1,698
			14 April		AMB Ltd	2,265
			14 April		D Draper	2,950
			22 April		Bank charges	63
			23 April		Overdraft fee	25
24 April	Balance c/d	1,191				
		22,618				**22,618**
			25 April		Balance b/d	1,191

21   WHOLESALE FLOORING

(a) – (c)

Date 20XX	Details	Bank £	Date 20XX	Cheque number	Details	Bank £
			01 June		Balance b/d	5,125
16 June	Beeston's	550	01 June	104373	Good Iron	890
19 June	Airfleet Exteriors	3,025	01 June	104374	Ashworth and Co	1,725
22 June	Jones's	2,775	01 June	104375	Ironfit	210
12 June	Aintree and Co	1,250	05 June	104376	OSS Ltd	1,275
			07 June	104377	Perfect Tools	725
			08 June	104378	Campden Ltd	784
			14 June	104379	Thornley and Thwaite	675
			14 June	104380	Castle and Cove	178
			20 June		MD County Council	400
			23 June		Bank charges	160
23 June	Balance c/d	4,637	23 June		Overdraft fee	90
		12,237				**12,237**
			24 June		Balance b/d	4,637

22   24 HOUR TAXIS

(a) – (c)

Date 20XX	Details	Bank £	Date 20XX	Cheque number	Details	Bank £
01 June	Balance b/d	6,025	01 June	102597	Best Ideas	910
18 June	Earnshaw's	1,000	02 June	102598	Bentley and Burn	2,010
19 June	Mainstreet Ltd	1,206	02 June	102599	Bits and Bats	315
21 June	Housley Inc	1,725	03 June	102600	LPF Ltd	1,725
12 June	Barron Homes	1,475	07 June	102601	Essentials	686
			08 June	102602	Hopburn Ltd	675
			15 June	102603	Thistle Tools	410
			15 June	102604	C Campbell Ltd	275
			20 June		AB Insurance	1,250
			23 June		Bank charges	50
			23 June		Overdraft fee	25
			23 June		Balance c/d	3,100
		11,431				11,431
24 June	Balance b/d	3,100				

23   WOOD

(a) – (c)

Date 20XX	Details	Bank £	Date 20XX	Cheque number	Details	Bank £
01 June	Balance b/d	17,640				
03 June	Bradley	1,320	04 June	110341	Carr	1,540
03 June	Cash sales	9,420	04 June	110342	Ramsden	980
03 June	Thanoj	2,450	04 June	110343	Coulson	750
21 June	Cash sales	7,430	04 June	110344	Brodie	570
21 June	Devitt	1,990	04 June	110345	Jones	550
17 June	Interest earned	80	04 June	110346	Gritton	740
			20 June		Bore	250
			12 June		Southwell	820
			20 June		Direct Debit Blundell	400
			23 June		Balance c/d	33,730
		40,330				40,330
24 June	Balance b/d	33,730				

24 CHANG

(a) – (c)

Date 20XX	Details	Bank £	Date 20XX	Cheque number	Details	Bank £
01 June	Balance b/d	550	07 June	110123	Connell	430
09 June	Cash sales	840	07 June	110124	Renner	720
14 June	Cash sales	1,540	07 June	110125	Bond	750
22 June	Cunnington	1,730	07 June	110126	Hatton	75
02 June	Interest received	5	07 June	110127	Bull	270
			07 June	110128	Black	135
			07 June	110129	Southall	740
			02 June		McMenemy	1,200
			20 June		Findus	300
			23 June		Bank charges	25
			23 June		Balance c/d	20
		4,665				**4,665**
24 June	Balance b/d	20				

25 MCKEOWN

(a) – (c)

Date 20XX	Details	Bank £	Date 20XX	Cheque number	Details	Bank £
01 June	Balance b/d	7,180	07 June	110157	Williams	430
12 June	Sherwood	640	07 June	110158	Forecast	520
14 June	Cash sales	1,200	07 June	110159	Beasant	1,240
22 June	Tweedy	860	07 June	110160	Davison	1,420
23 June	Butterwood	440	07 June	110161	Mildenhall	750
01 June	Interest received	85	23 June		Wilmott	300
20 June	Coyne	1,630				
23 June	Interest received	35				
			23 June		Balance c/d	7,410
		12,070				**12,070**
24 June	Balance b/d	7,410				

26   RIVERS BANK RECONCILIATION

Balance per bank statement	£510
Add:	
Name: Airfleet Interiors	£560
Name: Harris Homes	£333
Total to add	£893
Less:	
Name: OMD Ltd	£815
Name: Freeman & Cope	£522
Total to subtract	£1,337
Balance as per cash book	£66

27   LUXURY BATHROOMS BANK RECONCILIATION

Balance per bank statement	£82
Add:	
Name: Frith Ltd	£685
Name: Hodgetts & Co	£282
Total to add	£967
Less:	
Name: K Plomer	£542
Name: T Roberts	£1,698
Total to subtract	£2,240
Balance as per cash book	(£1,191)

28   WHOLESALE FLOORING BANK RECONCILIATION

Balance per bank statement	(£9,584)
Add:	
Name: Airfleet Exteriors	£3,025
Name: Jones's	£2,775
Total to add	£5,800
Less:	
Name: Thornley & Thwaite	£675
Name: Castle & Cove	£178
Total to subtract	£853
Balance as per cash book	(£4,637)

29   24 HOUR TAXIS BANK RECONCILIATION

Balance per bank statement	**£854**
Add:	
Name: Mainstreet Ltd	£1,206
Name: Housley Inc	£1,725
Total to add	**£2,931**
Less:	
Name: Thistle Tools	£410
Name: C Campbell Ltd	£275
Total to subtract	**£685**
Balance as per cash book	**£3,100**

30   WOOD BANK RECONCILIATION

(a)

Balance per bank statement	**£25,840**
Add:	
Name: Cash sales	£7,430
Name: Devitt	£1,990
Total to add	**£9,420**
Less:	
Name: Ramsden	£980
Name: Jones	£550
Total to subtract	**£1,530**
Balance as per cash book	**£33,730**

(b)

Balance carried down	**Bank column totals**
£	£
33,730	40,330

Working:

Cash book

Date 20XX	Details	Bank £	Date 20XX	Cheque number	Details	Bank £
01 June	Balance b/d	17,640				
03 June	Bradley	1,320	04 June	110341	Carr	1,540
03 June	Cash sales	9,420	04 June	110342	Ramsden	980
03 June	Thanoj	2,450	04 June	110343	Coulson	750
21 June	Cash sales	7,430	04 June	110344	Brodie	570
21 June	Devitt	1,990	04 June	110345	Jones	550
17 June	Interest earned	80	04 June	110346	Gritton	740
			20 June		Bore	250
			12 June		Southwell	820
			20 June		Direct Debit Blundell	400
			23 June		Balance c/d	33,730
		40,330				40,330
24 June	Balance b/d	33,730				

31 CHANG BANK RECONCILIATION

(a)

Balance per bank statement	(£105)
Add:	
Name: Cunnington	£1,730
Total to add	£1,730
Less:	
Name: Renner	£720
Name: Bond	£750
Name: Black	£135
Total to subtract	£1,605
Balance as per cash book	£20

(b) Show which security procedure listed below Chang should use to ensure the security of receipts from customers.

	✓
Cash received from customers should be kept in a locked safe until banked	✓
Cash should be banked on a monthly basis	
Cheques received too late to bank should be posted through the bank's letter box	

32   MCKEOWN BANK RECONCILIATION

(a)

Balance per bank statement	£8,770
Add:	
Name: Tweedy	£860
Name: Butterwood	£440
Total to add	**£1,300**
Less:	
Name: Beasant	£1,240
Name: Davison	£1,420
Total to subtract	**£2,660**
Balance as per cash book	**£7,410**

(b)

Balance carried down	Bank column totals
£	£
7,410	12,070

Workings:

Cash book

Date 20XX	Details	Bank £	Date 20XX	Cheque number	Details	Bank £
01 June	Balance b/d	7,180	07 June	110157	Williams	430
12 June	Sherwood	640	07 June	110158	Forecast	520
14 June	Cash sales	1,200	07 June	110159	Beasant	1,240
22 June	Tweedy	860	07 June	110160	Davison	1,420
23 June	Butterwood	440	07 June	110161	Mildenhall	750
01 June	Interest received	85	23 June		Wilmott	300
20 June	Coyne	1,630				
23 June	Interest received	35				
			23 June		Balance c/d	7,410
		12,070				12,070
24 June	Balance b/d	7,410				

USE THE JOURNAL

33   INTREPID INTERIORS

(a)

Account name	Amount £	Debit ✓	Credit ✓
Cash at bank	7,250	✓	
Bank Loan	5,000		✓
Capital	10,625		✓
Motor vehicles	4,750	✓	
Insurances	575	✓	
Stationery	300	✓	
Sundry expenses	225	✓	
Motor expenses	135	✓	
Advertising	990	✓	
Rent and rates	1,400	✓	

(b)

Recording of a contra

34   BITSY CAKES

(a)

Account name	Amount £	Debit ✓	Credit ✓
Cash	325	✓	
Cash at bank	9,625	✓	
Capital	22,008		✓
Fixtures and fittings	4,250	✓	
Insurance	1,050	✓	
Loan from bank	15,000		✓
Miscellaneous expenses	413	✓	
Motor vehicle	19,745	✓	
Office expenses	350	✓	
Rent and rates	1,250	✓	

(b)

Irrecoverable debt written off

35 GARAM GARDENS

Account name	Amount £	Debit ✓	Credit ✓
Cash	450	✓	
Cash at bank	11,125	✓	
Capital	28,941		✓
Plant and machinery	5,050	✓	
Insurance	990	✓	
Loan from bank	12,500		✓
General office expenses	378	✓	
Motor vehicle	20,755	✓	

36 IVANO

(a)

	Amount £
Net pay (2,400 – 480 – 245 – 80)	1,595

Note: The net pay is the gross pay less all the EMPLOYEE'S deductions. Employer's NIC is not part of this calculation.

(b)

	Amount £
Wages and salaries (Employer's expense) (2,400 Gross pay + 255 Employer's NIC)	2,655

(c)

	Amount £
Liabilities (HMRC and Pension) HMRC = 480 + 245 + 255 = 980 Pension = 80	1,060

37   ANNA

(a)

	Amount £
Net pay (1,400 – 280 – 125 – 60)	935

Note: The net pay is the gross pay less all the EMPLOYEE'S deductions. Employer's NIC is not part of this calculation.

(b)

	Amount £
Wages and salaries (Employer's expense) (1,400 Gross pay + 135 Employer's NIC + 70 Employer pension contributions)	1,605

(c)

	Amount £
Liabilities (HMRC and pension) HMRC = 280 + 125 + 135 = 540 Pension = 130	670

38   GROSS PAY 1

Item	Added to gross pay ✓	Not added to gross pay ✓
Trade Union subscription		✓
Employer's NIC	✓	
Employee's Pension		✓
Employer's Pension	✓	
Employee's NIC		✓

The wages expense comprises the employee's gross pay plus any contributions made by the employer, in this case pension and NIC. Trade Union subscription would be deducted from the employee's gross pay and paid to the Trade Union.

39 GROSS PAY 2

Item	Deducted from gross pay ✓	Not deducted from gross pay ✓
Employer's NIC		✓
Commission		✓
Employee's NIC	✓	
Employee pension contribution	✓	
PAYE	✓	

Gross pay is the amount the employee has earned from working for the company and therefore includes commission. Employer's NIC is added to gross pay in order to calculate the total wages expense for the company.

40 A POCKET FULL OF POSES

(i)

Account name	Amount £	Debit ✓	Credit ✓
Wages expense	17,755	✓	
Wages control	17,755		✓

(ii)

Account name	Amount £	Debit ✓	Credit ✓
Wages control	7,500	✓	
HMRC	7,500		✓

(iii)

Account name	Amount £	Debit ✓	Credit ✓
Wages control	8,405	✓	
Bank	8,405		✓

(iv)

Account name	Amount £	Debit ✓	Credit ✓
Wages control	1,850	✓	
Pension	1,850		✓

Proof (not required to answer the question correctly):

Wages control

HM Revenue and Customs	7,500	Wages expense	17,755
Bank	8,405		
Pension	1,850		
	17,755		17,755

41 RHYME TIME

(i)

Account name	Amount £	Debit ✓	Credit ✓
Wages expense	11,915	✓	
Wages control	11,915		✓

(ii)

Account name	Amount £	Debit ✓	Credit ✓
Wages control	5,026	✓	
HMRC	5,026		✓

(iii)

Account name	Amount £	Debit ✓	Credit ✓
Wages control	5,739	✓	
Bank	5,739		✓

(iv)

Account name	Amount £	Debit ✓	Credit ✓
Wages control	1,150	✓	
Pension	1,150		✓

Proof (not required to answer the question correctly):

Wages control

HMRC	5,026	Wages expense	11,915
Bank	5,739		
Pension	1,150		
	11,915		11,915

42 DOWN & OUT

(i)

Account name	Amount £	Debit ✓	Credit ✓
Wages expense	9,567	✓	
Wages control	9,567		✓

(ii)

Account name	Amount £	Debit ✓	Credit ✓
Wages control	3,673	✓	
HMRC	3,673		✓

(iii)

Account name	Amount £	Debit ✓	Credit ✓
Wages control	5,469	✓	
Bank	5,469		✓

(iv)

Account name	Amount £	Debit ✓	Credit ✓
Wages control	425	✓	
Trade union	425		✓

Proof (not required to answer the question correctly):

Wages control

HMRC	3,673	Wages expense	9,567
Bank	5,469		
Trade union	425		
	———		———
	9,567		9,567
	———		———

43   DEV

(i)

Account name	Amount £	Debit ✓	Credit ✓
Wages expense	13,963	✓	
Wages control	13,963		✓

(ii)

Account name	Amount £	Debit ✓	Credit ✓
Wages control	6,251	✓	
HMRC	6,251		✓

(iii)

Account name	Amount £	Debit ✓	Credit ✓
Wages control	7,212	✓	
Bank	7,212		✓

(iv)

Account name	Amount £	Debit ✓	Credit ✓
Wages control	500	✓	
Trade union	500		✓

Proof (not required to answer the question correctly):

Wages control

HMRC	6,251	Wages expense	13,963
Bank	7,212		
Trade Union	500		
	13,963		13,963

44   BEDROOM BITS

Account name	Amount £	Debit ✓	Credit ✓
Irrecoverable debts	2,000	✓	
VAT	400	✓	
Receivables ledger control	2,400		✓

45   GARDEN GATES

Account name	Amount £	Debit ✓	Credit ✓
Irrecoverable debts	2,600	✓	
VAT	520	✓	
Receivables ledger control	3,120		✓

46   CHESTNUT

RLCA

Details	Amount £	Details	Amount £
Balance b/d	46,000	Contra	4,000
		Balance c/d	42,000
	46,000		**46,000**
Balance b/d	42,000		

PLCA

Details	Amount £	Details	Amount £
Contra	4,000	Balance b/d	31,000
Balance c/d	27,000		
	31,000		**31,000**
		Balance b/d	27,000

47   ADELA

RLCA

Details	Amount £	Details	Amount £
Balance b/d	56,000	Contra	11,000
		Balance c/d	45,000
	56,000		**56,000**
Balance b/d	45,000		

PLCA

Details	Amount £	Details	Amount £
Contra	11,000	Balance b/d	49,000
Balance c/d	38,000		
	49,000		**49,000**
		Balance b/d	38,000

48   GANZ

Account name	Amount £	Debit ✓	Credit ✓
Irrecoverable debts	4,350	✓	
VAT	870	✓	
Receivables ledger control	5,220		✓

49   ERROR TYPES 1

Error in the general ledger	Error disclosed by the trial balance	Error NOT disclosed by the trial balance
Incorrectly calculating the balance on the Motor Vehicles account.	✓	
Recording a receipt for commission received in the bank interest received account.		✓
Recording a bank receipt for bank interest received on the debit side of both the bank account and the bank interest received account.	✓	
Recording supplier invoices on the debit side of the payables ledger control account and the credit side of the purchases account.		✓
Recording a payment by cheque to a payable in the payables ledger control account only.	✓	
Recording a bank payment of £124 for insurance as £142 in the insurance account and £124 in the bank account.	✓	

50 ERROR TYPES 2

Error in the general ledger	Would cause imbalance	Would NOT cause imbalance
Recording a bank receipt for rent received on the credit side of both the bank account and rent received account.	✓	
Recording a payment for new machinery in the equipment hire account.		✓
Recording a purchase return on the credit side of the payables ledger control account and the debit side of the purchase returns account.		✓
Incorrectly calculating the balance on the bank interest received account.	✓	
Recording a payment by cheque to a payable in the bank account only.	✓	
Recording a bank payment of £120 for stationery as £210 in both accounts.		✓

51 ERROR TYPES 3

Error in the general ledger	Type of error
Recording a bank receipt for rent received on the credit side of both the bank account and rent received account.	Two entries on one side
Recording a payment for new machinery in the equipment hire account.	Error of principle
Recording a purchase return on the credit side of the payables ledger control account and the debit side of the purchase returns account.	Reversal of entries

52 ERROR TYPES 4

Error in the general ledger	Type of error
Recording a payment by cheque to a payable in the bank account only.	Single entry
Recording a bank payment of £100 for stationery as £210 in both accounts.	Error of original entry
Recording a receipt for commission received in the bank interest received account.	Error of commission

53   ERROR TYPES 5

Error in the general ledger	Type of error
A credit sale made at the month end was not recorded.	Error of omission
Recording a bank payment of £120 for stationery as £210 in the stationery account and correctly in the bank account.	Transposition error
Recording a receipt for commission received in the PLCA.	Error of principle

54   ERROR TYPES 6

Error in the general ledger	Would cause imbalance ✓
Forgetting to post a journal to record a contra.	
Posting the VAT on a sale transaction as a debit rather than a credit.	✓
Recording a cash purchase in purchases and VAT only.	✓
Recording the electricity expense as a debit to wages expenses, with the corresponding entry correctly credited to cash.	

55   PRINCIPLES

(a)

Recording a bank payment for rent on the debit side of the office equipment account.	✓

(b)

Recording rent received as a debit in the rent account.	✓

56   EXTRACTION

(a)

Totalling the sales day book correctly but entering into the RLCA as a credit balance.	✓

(b)

Posting a £200 invoice for electricity as £210 in both the electricity and bank account.	✓

57   BANK ERROR

(i)

Account name	Amount £	Debit ✓	Credit ✓
Repairs	750	✓	
Bank	750		✓

(ii)

Account name	Amount £	Debit ✓	Credit ✓
Repairs	750	✓	
Bank	750		✓

58   RENT ERROR

(i)

Account name	Amount £	Debit ✓	Credit ✓
Bank	500	✓	
Rent received	500		✓

(ii)

Account name	Amount £	Debit ✓	Credit ✓
Bank	500	✓	
Rent received	500		✓

59   GAS ERROR

Account name	Amount £	Debit ✓	Credit ✓
Gas expenses	300	✓	
Electricity expenses	300		✓

60   BUILDING ERROR

Account name	Amount £	Debit ✓	Credit ✓
Suspense	360,000	✓	
Bank	360,000		✓

61   SALES ERROR

Account name	Amount £	Debit ✓	Credit ✓
Sales	2,000	✓	
VAT	2,000		✓

62   MOTOR ERROR

Account name	Amount £	Debit ✓	Credit ✓
Motor expenses	700	✓	
Motor vehicles	700		✓

63   INVENTORY ERROR

Account name	Amount £	Debit ✓	Credit ✓
Purchases	375	✓	
VAT	75	✓	
Payables ledger control	450		✓

64   SUBSCRIPTIONS ERROR

Account name	Amount £	Debit ✓	Credit ✓
Subscriptions expense	160	✓	
Bank	160		✓

65   PURCHASE ERROR

Account name	Amount £	Debit ✓	Credit ✓
VAT	1,500	✓	
Purchases	1,500		✓

66   INSURANCE ERROR

Account name	Amount £	Debit ✓	Credit ✓
Payables ledger control	2,700	✓	
Bank	2,700		✓

67   CB INTERIORS

(i)

Account name	Amount £	Debit ✓	Credit ✓
Payables ledger control	960	✓	

(ii)

Account name	Amount £	Debit ✓	Credit ✓
Payables ledger control	9,600		✓

(iii)

Account name	Amount £	Debit ✓	Credit ✓
Suspense	8,640	✓	

68   ROGER DODGER

(i)

Account name	Amount £	Debit ✓	Credit ✓
VAT	1,680	✓	

(ii)

Account name	Amount £	Debit ✓	Credit ✓
VAT	1,320		✓

(iii)

Account name	Amount £	Debit ✓	Credit ✓
Suspense	360		✓

69 A CUT ABOVE

(i)

Account name	Amount £	Debit ✓	Credit ✓
Payables ledger control	6,182		✓

(ii)

Account name	Amount £	Debit ✓	Credit ✓
Payables ledger control	5,952	✓	

(iii)

Account name	Amount £	Debit ✓	Credit ✓
Suspense	230	✓	

70 RESTCO

(i)

Account name	Amount £	Debit ✓	Credit ✓
Sales	8,080	✓	

(ii)

Account name	Amount £	Debit ✓	Credit ✓
Sales	8,800		✓

(iii)

Account name	Amount £	Debit ✓	Credit ✓
Suspense	720	✓	

71 JOHNNY JOINER

(a)

Account name	Amount £	Debit ✓	Credit ✓
Suspense	14,363		✓

(b)

Account name	Amount £	Debit ✓	Credit ✓
Suspense	14,363	✓	
Sales	14,363		✓

72 BUCKLEY DRAINS

(a)

Account name	Amount £	Debit ✓	Credit ✓
Suspense	10,805		✓

(b)

Account name	Amount £	Debit ✓	Credit ✓
Suspense	10,805	✓	
Payables ledger control	10,805		✓

(c)   Show one reason for maintaining the journal

	✓
To correct errors only	
To correct errors and record transactions that have not been recorded in any other book of prime entry	✓
To record transactions from every other book of prime entry.	

73 MENDONCA

(a)

Account name	Amount £	Debit ✓	Credit ✓
Suspense	1,980		✓

(b)

Account name	Amount £	Debit ✓	Credit ✓
Suspense	1,980	✓	
Wages	900	✓	
Bank	2,880		✓

74 BEASANT

(a)

Account name	Amount £	Debit ✓	Credit ✓
Suspense	15,000		✓

(b)

Account name	Amount £	Debit ✓	Credit ✓
Suspense	15,000	✓	
Sales	12,500		✓
VAT	2,500		✓

(c)   Show one reason for maintaining the journal

	✓
To detect fraud	
To record non-regular transactions	✓
To record goods sold on credit	

75   PAT'S CAFE

(a)   What entry would be made in the suspense account to balance the trial balance?

Account name	Amount £	Debit ✓	Credit ✓
Suspense	4,650	✓	

(b)

Account name	Balance £	Debit ✓	Credit ✓
Bank interest paid	235	✓	
Bank interest received	61		✓
Insurance	550	✓	
Motor vehicles	6,500	✓	

76   TWINKLE'S TRINKETS

(a)

Account name	Amount £	Debit ✓	Credit ✓
Suspense	776		✓

(b)

Account name	Balance £	Debit ✓	Credit ✓
Motor expenses	8,744	✓	
Repairs and renewals	1,210	✓	
Rent payable	3,700	✓	
Rent received	1,700		✓

77   SPARKS AND MENCER

Account name	Balance £	Debit ✓	Credit ✓
Heat and light	655	✓	
Rates	1,416	✓	
Loan interest expense	165	✓	
Rent received	119		✓

PRODUCE THE TRIAL BALANCE

78   RAVI'S RACERS

		Balances at 1 July	
		Debit	Credit £
Motor vehicles	24,200	✓	
Plant and equipment	22,350	✓	
Inventory	9,000	✓	
Cash at bank	11,217	✓	
Cash	150	✓	
Receivables ledger control	131,275	✓	
Payables ledger control	75,336		✓
VAT owing to HM Revenue and Customs	15,127		✓
Capital	26,247		✓
Bank loan	12,500		✓
Sales	276,132		✓
Purchases	152,476	✓	
Wages	35,465	✓	
Motor expenses	3,617	✓	
Repairs and renewals	2,103	✓	
Rent and rates	3,283	✓	
Light and heat	4,012	✓	
Insurance	4,874	✓	
Sundry expenses	1,320	✓	
Suspense account (credit balance)			

79   PERCY POTS

	Balances at 1 July	
	Debit £	Credit £
Motor vehicles	22,348	
Fixtures and fittings	9,234	
Inventory	4,800	
Bank		2,661
Petty cash	100	
Receivables ledger control	61,025	
Payables ledger control		35,275
VAT owing to HM Revenue and Customs		4,630
Capital		4,852
Sales		142,378
Sales returns	1,870	
Purchases	69,276	
Wages	13,500	
Motor expenses	873	
Office expenses	1,796	
Rent and rates	1,276	
Heat and light	1,022	
Insurance	1,629	
Miscellaneous expenses	1,047	
Suspense account		
Total	**189,796**	**189,796**

80   IVOR ISLAND

	Balances extracted on 30 April	Balances at 1 May	
		Debit £	Credit £
Motor vehicles	8,454	8,454	
Office building	28,676	28,676	
Inventory	15,369	15,369	
Bank	26,984	26,984	
Petty cash	459	459	
Receivables ledger control	35,987	35,987	
Payables ledger control	26,942		26,942
VAT (owing to HM Revenue and Customs)	231		(W1) 941
Capital	98,106		98,106
Sales	96,325		96,325
Purchase returns	3,654		(W2) 3,954
Purchases	68,975	68,975	
Wages	18,564	18,564	
Motor expenses	1,269	1,269	
Office expenses	5,798	5,798	
Rates	4,300	4,300	
Heat and light	5,423	5,423	
Insurance	3,365	3,365	
Misc. expenses	2,645	2,645	
Suspense account (credit balance)	1,472	nil	nil
Totals		**226,268**	**226,268**

Workings:

(W1)

VAT

Details	Amount £	Details	Amount £
Balance b/f	231	Suspense	586
		Suspense	586
Balance c/d	941		
	1,172		**1,172**
		Balance b/d	941

(W2)

Purchase returns

Details	Amount £	Details	Amount £
Suspense	2,256	Balance b/d	3,654
		Suspense	2,556
Balance c/d	3,954		
	6,210		**6,210**
		Balance b/d	3,954

81   RING OF ROSES

	Balances at 1 July	
	Debit £	Credit £
Motor vehicles	27,625	
Plant and equipment	5,000	
Inventory	7,350	
Cash at bank	14,345	
Cash	200	
Receivables ledger control	121,275	
Payables ledger control		67,323
VAT owing to HM Revenue and Customs		10,098
Capital		22,291
Sales		253,727
Sales returns	2,123	
Purchases	134,931	
Purchase returns		9,872
Wages	34,250	
Motor expenses	1,797	
Office expenses	4,946	
Rent and rates	2,321	
Heat and light	3,123	
Insurance	4,025	
Suspense account		
Total	**363,311**	**363,311**

82   HEARN

Journal entries

Account name	Debit £	Credit £
Rent	90	
Suspense		90
VAT	120	
Suspense		120

| | Balances extracted on 30 June £ | Balances at 1 July | |
		Debit £	Credit £
Receivables ledger control	34,560	34,560	
Payables ledger control	21,420		21,420
VAT owing to HM Revenue and Customs	3,412		3,292
Capital	50,000		50,000
Sales	201,327		201,327
Sales returns	1,465	1,465	
Purchases	87,521	87,521	
Purchase returns	252		252
Plant and equipment	15,200	15,200	
Motor expenses	4,310	4,310	
Office expenses	10,321	10,321	
Rent and rates	21,420	21,510	
Heat and light	8,920	8,920	
Wages	53,205	53,205	
Irrecoverable debt	1,450	1,450	
Office equipment	42,030	42,030	
Bank overdraft	4201		4201
Suspense account (debit balance)	210		
Totals		280,492	280,492

83   RODMAN

Journal entries

Account name	Debit £	Credit £
Suspense	1,250	
VAT		1,250
Wages	8,600	
Suspense		8,600

	Balances extracted on 30 June £	Balances at 1 July	
		Debit £	Credit £
Receivables ledger control	38,070	38,070	
Payables ledger control	20,310		20,310
VAT owed from HM Revenue and Customs	2,510	1,260	
Capital	70,000		70,000
Sales	153,488		153,488
Sales returns	2,135	2,135	
Purchases	63,261	63,261	
Purchase returns	542		542
Plant and equipment	17,319	17,319	
Motor expenses	3,214	3,214	
Office expenses	6,421	6,421	
Rent and rates	17,414	17,414	
Heat and light	6,421	6,421	
Wages	45,532	54,132	
Irrecoverable debt	1,532	1,532	
Office equipment	35,313	35,313	
Bank overdraft	2,152		2,152
Suspense account (debit balance)	7,350		
Totals		246,492	246,492

84   SMITH & SON

Account name	Amount £	Debit £	Credit £
Fixtures and fittings	8,250	8,250	
Capital	18,400		18,400
Bank overdraft	4,870		4,870
Petty cash control	350	350	
Receivables ledger control (RLCA)	42,870	42,870	
Payables ledger control (PLCA)	23,865		23,865
VAT owed to tax authorities	10,245		10,245
Inventory	9,870	9,870	
Loan from bank	22,484		22,484
Sales	180,264		180,264
Sales returns	5,420	5,420	
Purchases	129,030	129,030	
Purchases returns	2,678		2,678
Discount allowed	2,222	2,222	
Discount received	3,432		3,432
Heat and Light	1,490	1,490	
Motor expenses	2,354	2,354	
Wages	42,709	42,709	
Rent and rates	10,600	10,600	
Repairs	3,020	3,020	
Hotel expenses	1,890	1,890	
Telephone	2,220	2,220	
Delivery costs	1,276	1,276	
Miscellaneous expenses	2,667	2,667	
Totals	532,476	266,238	266,238

85 EXPIALIDOCIOUS LTD

Account name	Amount £	Debit £	Credit £
Capital	25,360		25,360
Petty cash control	250	250	
Loan from bank	11,600		11,600
Receivables ledger control (RLCA)	159,242	159,242	
Payables ledger control (PLCA)	83,682		83,682
Motor vehicles	35,900	35,900	
Inventory	28,460	28,460	
Bank overdraft	10,063		10,063
VAT owed from tax authorities	15,980	15,980	
Purchases	343,014	343,014	
Purchases returns	1,515		1,515
Wages	56,150	56,150	
Motor expenses	2,950	2,950	
Interest income	400		400
Sales	532,900		532,900
Sales returns	5,760	5,760	
Stationery	1,900	1,900	
Light & heat	6,500	6,500	
Discount received	200		200
Discount allowed	2,160	2,160	
Interest paid on overdraft	550	550	
Travel	1,800	1,800	
Marketing	650	650	
Telephone	1,510	1,510	
Miscellaneous expenses	2,944	2,944	
Totals		665,720	665,720

86   DIXON FURNITURE

Account name	Amount £	Debit £	Credit £
Motor vehicles	40,100	40,100	
Capital	35,000		35,000
Petty cash control	150	150	
Bank balance	14,654	14,654	
Wages	37,890	37,890	
Travel expenses	1,500	1,500	
Rental income	1,000		1,000
Sales	435,600		435,600
Loan from bank	10,000		10,000
Receivables ledger control (RLCA)	127,456	127,456	
Inventory	22,500	22,500	
Payables ledger control (PLCA)	91,250		91,250
VAT due to tax authorities	12,500		12,500
Purchases	325,600	325,600	
Sales returns	6,500	6,500	
Purchases returns	1,250		1,250
Sundry expenses	3,600	3,600	
Electricity expense	450	450	
Bank interest received	360		360
Fuel expense	900	900	
Discount received	600		600
Discount allowed	1,560	1,560	
Advertising	300	300	
Telephone	1,900	1,900	
Miscellaneous expenses	2,500	2,500	
Totals		587,560	587,560

87   **ARCHIE**

(a)   Calculate the total of each of the debit and credit columns of the partially complete trial balance.

Debit £	Credit £
115,435	111,811

(b)   Transfer each balance to the debit or credit column of the trial balance extract below.

Account name	Debit £	Credit £
Drawings	2,350	
Payables ledger control		6,859
Discounts allowed	885	

(c)   Calculate the final total to be entered into the debit and credit columns of the trial balance.

£118,670

(d)   Identify SIX accounts that will appear in the trial balance and whether they will be transferred to the debit or credit column.

Account name	Debit ✓	Credit ✓	Does not appear in the trial balance ✓
Fixtures and fittings	✓		
Capital		✓	
Discounts allowed	✓		
Rent received		✓	
Bank	✓		
Sales		✓	
Original Ltd			✓
Evie & Joe			✓
Jacob & Danny			✓
PPR LLP			✓

88   HARRISON

(a)   Calculate the total of each of the debit and credit columns of the partially complete trial balance.

Debit £	Credit £
109,155	113,390

(b)   Transfer each balance to the debit or credit column of the trial balance extract below.

Account name	Debit £	Credit £
Drawings	8,000	
Capital		3,315
Discounts received		450

(c)   Calculate the final total to be entered into the debit and credit columns of the trial balance.

£117,155

(d)   Identify SIX accounts that will appear in the trial balance and whether they will be transferred to the debit or credit column

Account name	Debit ✓	Credit ✓	Does not appear in the trial balance ✓
Motor vehicles	✓		
Capital		✓	
Discounts received		✓	
Interest paid	✓		
Bank overdraft		✓	
Purchases	✓		
Dave & Malc Co			✓
Amy & Molly			✓
Peter & Paul			✓
Morris Ltd			✓

89   KOOKABURRA

(a)   Calculate and insert the total of each of the debit and credit columns of the partially prepared trial balance.

Account name	Debit £	Credit £
Plant and equipment	106,340	
Receivables ledger control (RLCA)	36,470	
Bank	12,590	
Inventory	18,240	
Payables ledger control (PLCA)		27,021
Capital		50,000
Bank loan		2,590
Sales		625,640
Purchases	295,100	
Wages	32,410	
Administrative expenses	1,280	
Rent and rates	12,490	
Heat and light	4,291	
Entertainment expenses	456	
Telephone and broadband expenses	3,214	
Totals	522,881	705,251

(b)   Transfer each balance to the debit or credit column of the trial balance extract below.

Account name	Amount £	Debit £	Credit £
Purchases returns	14,980		14,980
Land and Buildings	197,000	197,000	
Petty cash	350	350	

(c)   Calculate the final total entered into the debit and credit columns of the trial balance.

£720,231

(d) You are required to identify whether these accounts appear in the trial balance and if so whether they would be transferred to the debit or credit column.

Receivables ledger

Account name	Account balance	Transfers to the trial balance in the DEBIT column ✓	Transfers to the trial balance in the CREDIT column ✓	Does not transfer to the trial balance ✓
Riley Racing	£3,250			✓
Kat's Cakes	£2,560			✓

Payables ledger

Account name	Account balance	Transfers to the trial balance in the DEBIT column ✓	Transfers to the trial balance in the CREDIT column ✓	Does not transfer to the trial balance ✓
VK Supplies	£2,364			✓
TAF Ltd	£7,171			✓

General ledger

Account name	Account balance	Transfers to the trial balance in the DEBIT column ✓	Transfers to the trial balance in the CREDIT column ✓	Does not transfer to the trial balance ✓
Sales returns	£23,910	✓		
Bank overdraft	£2,185		✓	

90   ALAN

(a)   If Alan's trial balance balances, what is the missing figure for the receivables ledger control?

B   £111,000

Working:

Account	Debit £	Credit £
Sales		628,000
Cost of sales	458,000	
General expenses	138,000	
Payables ledger control		54,000
Receivables ledger control (balancing figure)	111,000	
Bank (in funds)	61,000	
Capital		86,000
Totals	**768,000**	**768,000**

(b)   Taking into consideration the answer to part (a) what is the trial balance total?

£768,000   See working in part (a).

(c)   Which of the following balances would appear on the same side in the trial balance?

B   Assets, expenses and drawings are debit balances in the trial balance.

Section 3

MOCK ASSESSMENT QUESTIONS

TASK 1   **(10 MARKS)**

This task is about using control accounts.

This task contains parts (a) to (c).

A payables ledger control account is shown in the general ledger.

(a)   **Identify which ONE of the following is correct in relation to the payables ledger control account.**

	✓
A payables ledger control account includes accounting entries for irrecoverable debts written off.	
A contra between the payables ledger control account and the receivables ledger control account will increase the balance on both control accounts	
The payables ledger control account does not include cash purchases.	
The payables ledger control account includes accounting for discounts allowed.	

You work in the accounts department of Target Ltd. Your manager has run a report, which shows a credit balance on the VAT control account at the end of June of £8,573. The credit balance at the end of July was £10,324. Your manager has asked you to prepare a VAT control account to explain why July shows a higher balance.

The following information has been recorded for the month of July:

Item	£
VAT on purchases	8,614
VAT on purchases returns	1,985
VAT on sales	13,462
VAT on sales returns	121
VAT on discounts allowed	75
VAT on discounts received	57
VAT on cash sales	3,630
Payment made to HMRC	8,573

(b) Complete the VAT control account below for July by selecting an entry from each pick list and entering amounts in the spaces provided. You must ensure that a number is entered in each space provided. **(8 marks)**

VAT Control Account

Details	Amount £	Details	Amount £
		Balance b/d	8,573
Balance c/d	10,324		

Select your account names from the following list: Purchases, Purchases returns, Sales, Sales returns, Discounts allowed, Discounts received, Bank, Cash sales

Canter Ltd has the following receivables ledger control account:

Receivables ledger control

Details	Amount £	Details	Amount £
Balance b/d	36,750	Sales returns	1,345
Sales	45,450	Bank	30,234
		Discounts allowed	632
		Contra with payables ledger control	2,050
		Irrecoverable debts	1,640
		Balance c/d	

(c) What will be the balance carried down on the receivables ledger control account?

(1 mark)

£ [   ]

TASK 2 (10 MARKS)

This task is about reconciling control accounts.

This task contains parts (a) to (c).

A payables ledger control account is shown in the general ledger.

(a) **Identify which ONE of the following statements is true in relation to this reconciliation.**

	✓
A payables ledger control account confirms that the value of contras with the receivables ledger control account is correct.	
A contra between the payables ledger control account and the receivables ledger control account will decrease the balance on both control accounts.	
The payables ledger control account includes payments made by petty cash.	
The payables ledger control account includes accounting entries for discounts allowed.	

You work in the accounts department of Astro Ltd. Your manager has asked you to reconcile the balance on the payables ledger control account with the listing of payables ledger account balances. Your manager provided the following report dated 30 November:

Payable account	£
Arable Brothers	5,250
Gardening Requirements Ltd	8,310
Gnomes4U Ltd	18,760
Grass Supplies Ltd	14,871
Horticulture Partnership	1,842
Seeds & Sprays Ltd	3,750

(b) **(i)** **If the payables ledger control balance reconciles with the payables ledger, what will be the balance?**

£

The balance on the payables ledger control account is £51,893

(ii) **Complete the following statement:**

The payables ledger control account is £……………higher/lower* than the payables ledger. (*delete which is not applicable.)

The receivables ledger control account shows a balance of £84,628, but the individual balances in the receivables ledger total £82,862.

(c)   Identify whether each of the following may explain the difference between the two balances.

Reason	May explain the difference	Does not explain the difference
The receivables ledger control account includes entries for contras with the payables ledger control account, which are not, recorded in the receivables ledger accounts.		
The receivables ledger accounts include entries for discounts allowed which have not been recorded in the receivables ledger control account.		
The receivables ledger accounts include entries for sales returns which are not included in the receivables ledger control account.		
Several sales invoices were recorded twice in the receivables ledger accounts.		
Irrecoverable debts written off had been recorded in the receivables ledger accounts, but not included on the receivables ledger control account.		

TASK 3 (8 MARKS)

This task is about payment methods and reconciling the cash book to the bank statement.

This task contains parts (a) to (c).

A payables ledger control account is shown in the general ledger.

(a)   **Insert one payment method for each description from the pick list below.**

Description	Payment method
An electronic system to make payments directly from one bank account to another. They're mainly used for direct debits and direct credits. Transfers usually take three working days.	
A UK-based system that enables almost instantaneous transfer of large funds denominated in UK sterling between banks and other financial institutions.	
A plastic card that is issued by a bank allowing the holder to purchase goods or services on credit.	
An instruction to a bank by an account holder authorising the organisation the account holder wants to pay, to collect varying amounts from the account. Advanced notice of the amounts and dates of collection must be given.	

Select your payment method from the following list: BACS, Cash, CHAPS, Cheque, Credit Card, Debit card, Direct debit, Standing order.

(b)   Which ONE of the following statements is true?

	✓
The balance on the bank statement will always be lower than the cash book balance when a bank reconciliation is performed.	
At the date a bank reconciliation is performed, there may be a debit balance on the bank statement and a debit balance in the cash book.	
At the year end, the balance on the bank statement will be included in the trial balance.	

(c)   Identify whether each of the following statements is true or false:

	True	False
A payment omitted from the cash book and not included in the bank statement is an example of a timing difference.		
A timing difference will always increase the cash book balance.		
If uncleared lodgements have been identified when performing a bank reconciliation, the cash book will not need to be updated.		

TASK 4   (12 MARKS)

This task is about reconciling a bank statement with the cash book.

The cash book for Lee's car spares business at 30 April is shown below. Lee pays out all suppliers by cheque and all customers pay Lee by either cheque or bank transfer.

(a)   Update the cash book and calculate the closing balance.

On 3 May Lee received the following bank statement as at 30 April.

ZYX Bank plc 68 London Road, Reading, RG8 4RN					
To: Lee's Car Spares		Account No: 55548921		30 April 20XX	
		Statement of Account			
Date	**Detail**	**Paid out**	**Paid in**	**Balance**	
20XX		**£**	**£**	**£**	
03 April	Balance b/d			18,000	C
03 April	Cheque 120045	6,234		11,766	C
04 April	Bank Giro Priceright		342	12,108	C
04 April	Cheque 120046	1,632		10,476	C
05 April	Cheque 120047	41		10,435	C
08 April	Cheque 120048	4,444		5,991	C
14 April	Direct debit Steering Ltd	2,878		3,113	C
14 April	Direct debit Steamcar	2,865		248	C
14 April	Cheque 120050	432		184	D
22 April	Paid in at SKB Bank		5,321	5,137	C
29 April	Bank charges	54		5,083	C
29 April	Overdraft fee	27		5,056	C
D = Debit C = Credit					

The cash book as at 30 April is shown below.

Cash Book

Date	Details	Bank	Date	Cheque	Details	Bank
01 April	Balance b/d	18,000	01 April	120045	Mose Ltd	6,234
19 April	Wallace	5,321	01 April	120046	Sabre	1,632
28 April	Bennett	685	01 April	120047	Hannan	41
29 April	Lewis	282	02 April	120048	Flinderson	4,444
			02 April	120049	Bratton	542
			08 April	120050	Falcon	432
			08 April	120051	Vickers	1,698
			24 April	DD	Steering	2,878

Details column options: Balance b/d, balance c/d, Bank charges, Mose Ltd, Sabre, Hannan, Steamcar, Flinderson, Bratton, Falcon, Vickers, Wallace, Bennett, Lewis, Priceright, Opening balance, Steering Overdraft fees

(b) **Complete the bank reconciliation statement for Lee's Car Spares Ltd for 30 April.**

Balance per bank statement	£5056
Outstanding lodgements	
Name:	£
Name:	£
Unpresented cheques	
Name:	£
Name:	£
Balance as per cash book	£

TASK 5 (10 MARKS)

This task is about using the journal.

This task contains parts (a) to (c).

(a) **Identify which TWO of the following situations would be a correct use of the journal.**

	✓
Rayyan made a payment of VAT to HMR&C and recorded this transaction in the journal.	
Zein has a receivable which has been outstanding for two months and wishes to make an allowance for a doubtful debt. Zein recorded the increase in the allowance for doubtful debts in the journal.	
Nour incurred bank fees and charges. The fees and charges were recorded in the journal.	
Farah calculated the annual depreciation charge on the delivery van used in the business. Details of the depreciation charge were recorded in the journal.	

A journal has been recorded in the accounting system as follows:

Account name	Debit £	Credit £
Payroll expenses – wages (Gross pay)	35,842	
Payroll liabilities – HMRC (Employer national insurance)		2,900
Payroll liabilities – HMRC (Employee national insurance)		3,419
Payroll expenses – taxes (Employer national insurance)	2,900	
Payroll liabilities – HMRC (PAYE)		3,725
Payroll expenses – employees (Net pay)		28,698

Prior to this journal, the balance on the Payroll liabilities – HMRC account was a debit balance of £85.

(b) **After the journals are processed, what will be the revised balance on the Payroll liabilities – HMRC account?**

£ [   ]

Prototype & Co

5 Pheasant Way, Essex, ES9 8BN

VAT Registration No. 453 098 541

Invoice No. 2176

Marco Ltd

9 Banbury Street

Sheffield

1 July 20XX

10 of Power drill and bit set (Product code PD999) @ £480 each	£4,800
Twelve month guarantee	£300
Total (including £850 VAT @ 20%)	£5,100
Payment terms: 30 days	

(c)   **Complete the journal entries below to record the purchase of the drill and bit sets.**

Account name	Debit £	Credit £

Account names column options: Bank, Depreciation expense, Non-current asset, Payable, Receivable, Repairs and maintenance, VAT

TASK 6   (10 MARKS)

This task is about using the journal to correct errors.

This task contains parts (a) to (c).

(a)   **Identify which TWO of the following statements about suspense accounts are true?**

(2 marks)

	✓
If the value of a transaction was transposed from £963 to £693 when both the debit and credit entries were posted into the ledger accounts, this not will require a suspense account to be opened.	
A suspense account is used to record accounting for the depreciation expense for the year.	
If the totals of the trial balance do not agree, one possible reason for this will be that a ledger balance has been omitted.	
A suspense account will normally be part of the initial trial balance for a business at the start of the accounting year.	

(b) Identify whether each of the errors described below would or would not be disclosed in the trial balance. **(2 marks)**

Error in the general ledger	Error disclosed by the trial balance ✓	Error NOT disclosed by the trial balance ✓
Recording a bank payment for purchases on the debit side of both the bank and purchases account.		
Recording a payment for rent and rates in a non-current assets account.		

Paolo and Marina run a general hardware supplies business and operate a manual accounting system. A trial balance was prepared for the business as at 30 September and it has total debits of £57,636 and total credits of £57,610. A suspense account was included in the trial balance.

Following an investigation, the following errors were identified:

Error in the general ledger	
1	A photocopier was purchased at a cost of £810 plus VAT at 20%. The payable had been recorded correctly, as had the cost of the net cost of the photocopier. The VAT element had been credited to the VAT account.
2	During the year, the business sold its delivery van at a profit of £175. The profit on disposal was included in the trial balance as a debit balance.

(c) **(i)** What is the balance on the suspense account in the trial balance? **(2 marks)**

£	Debit/Credit

(ii) Complete the table below to show the debits and credits that will be processed to clear the suspense account. **(4 marks)**

Error 1 Account name	£	Debit ✓	Credit ✓
VAT	324		
Suspense	324		
Error 2 Account name			
Suspense	350		
Profit on disposal of van	350		

Account names column options: Bank, Depreciation expense, Non-current asset, Payable, Receivable, Repairs and maintenance, VAT

TASK 7   **(10 MARKS)**

This task is about extracting a trial balance.

This task contains parts (a) to (b).

Varuna runs a business that sells sports clothes and equipment. Most of the ledger accounts have been closed off and the balances are included in the trial balance as at 31 October.

(a)   **Complete the remaining ledger accounts by inserting the balance carried down on each account.**   **(4 marks)**

Receivables ledger control

Details	Amount £	Details	Amount £
Balance b/d	5,750	Sales returns	345
Sales	12,450	Bank	8,234
		Discounts allowed	32
		Contra with payables ledger control	1,950
		Irrecoverable debts	940
		Balance c/d	

HMRC – tax and insurance liabilities

Details	Amount £	Details	Amount £
Balance b/d	75	PAYE	1,345
Bank	3,450	Employer NI	1,128
Balance c/d		Employee NI	1,208

Payables ledger control

Details	Amount £	Details	Amount £
Purchases returns	827	Balance b/d	4,345
Discounts received	252	Purchases	8,450
Bank	4,273		
Contra with receivables ledger control	1,950		
Balance c/d			

Repairs and maintenance

Details	Amount £	Details	Amount £
Bank	365		
Bank	142		
Petty cash	13	Balance c/d	

(b) Complete the trial balance by inserting the missing figures and calculating the total for each column. (6 marks)

Balances at 31 October	Debit £	Credit £
Sales		14,450
Purchases	8,450	
Admin expenses	1,209	
Irrecoverable debt expense	940	
Payables ledger control account		
Repairs and maintenance		
Capital account		6,638
Inventory	3,268	
Receivables ledger control account		
Discounts received		252
Bank	1,923	
HMRC – tax and insurance liabilities		
Wages expense	8,980	
Bank loan		5,000
Totals		

TASK 8   **(10 MARKS)**

This task is about redrafting the trial balance.

Rei has extracted a list of balances at 31 December as follows:

	£
Sales	279,082
Purchases	183,593
Opening inventory	21,211
Payroll expenses	61,326
General expenses	24,790
Capital account	15,710
Receivables ledger control	22,642
Payables ledger control	15,566
Bank (overdrawn)	2,510
VAT liability	2,529

Some errors have been identified and the following journals are required to be posted:

Journal – 31 December	Debit £	Credit £
Suspense	1,890	
General expenses		1,890
General Expenses paid recorded as £1,234 recorded as £3,124 within expense account.		
Receivables ledger control	3,725	
Suspense		3,725
Several invoices for sales made on credit had been correctly recorded in the sales account, but no other accounting entry had been made.		

Complete the adjusted trial balance by inserting the correct figures in either the debit or credit column and entering columns for each total.

Trial Balance as at 31 December	Dr £	Cr £
Sales		
Purchases		
Opening inventory		
Payroll expenses		
General expenses		
Capital account		
Receivables ledger control		
Payables ledger control		
Bank		
VAT		
Total		

Section 4

MOCK ASSESSMENT ANSWERS

TASK 1 **(10 MARKS)**

(a)

	✓
A payables ledger control account includes accounting entries for irrecoverable debts written off.	
A contra between the payables ledger control account and the receivables ledger control account will increase the balance on both control accounts	
The payables ledger control account does not include cash purchases.	✓
The payables ledger control account includes accounting for discounts allowed.	

(b)

VAT control account

Details	Amount £	Details	Amount £
Sales returns	121	Balance b/d	8,573
Purchases	8,614	Sales	13,462
Bank	8,573	Cash sales	3,630
Discounts allowed	75	Purchases returns	1,985
Balance c/d	10,324	Discounts received	57
	27,707		27,707

(c)

Receivables ledger control

Details	Amount £	Details	Amount £
Balance b/d	36,750	Sales returns	1,345
Sales	45,450	Bank	30,234
		Discounts allowed	632
		Contra with payables ledger control	2,050
		Irrecoverable debts	1,640
		Balance c/d	46,299
	82,200		**82,200**

TASK 2 (10 MARKS)

(a)

	✓
A payables ledger control account confirms that the value of contras with the receivables ledger control account is correct.	
A contra between the payables ledger control account and the receivables ledger control account will decrease the balance on both control accounts.	✓
The payables ledger control account includes payments made by petty cash.	
The payables ledger control account includes accounting entries for discounts allowed.	

(b) (i)

Payable account	£
Arable Brothers	5,250
Gardening Requirements Ltd	8,310
Gnomes4U Ltd	18,760
Grass Supplies Ltd	14,871
Horticulture Partnership	1,842
Seeds & Sprays Ltd	3,750
Total	52,783

(ii) The payables ledger control account is £890 lower than the payables ledger.

(c)

Reason	May explain the difference	Does not explain the difference
The receivables ledger control account includes entries for contras with the payables ledger control account which are not recorded in the receivables ledger accounts.		✓
The receivables ledger accounts include entries for discounts allowed which have not been recorded in the receivables ledger control account.	✓	
The receivables ledger accounts include entries for sales returns which are not included in the receivables ledger control account.	✓	
Several sales invoices were recorded twice in the receivables ledger accounts.		✓
Irrecoverable debts written off had been recorded in the receivables ledger accounts, but not included on the receivables ledger control account.	✓	

TASK 3 (8 MARKS)

(a)

Description	Payment method
An electronic system to make payments directly from one bank account to another. They're mainly used for direct debits and direct credits. Transfers usually take three working days.	**BACS**
A UK-based system that enables almost instantaneous transfer of large funds denominated in UK sterling between banks and other financial institutions.	**CHAPS**
A plastic card that is issued by a bank allowing the holder to purchase goods or services on credit.	**Credit card**
An instruction to a bank by an account holder authorising the organisation the account holder wants to pay, to collect varying amounts from the account. Advanced notice of the amounts and dates of collection must be given.	**Direct debit**

(b)

	✓
The balance on the bank statement will always be lower than the cash book balance when a bank reconciliation is performed.	
At the date a bank reconciliation is performed, there may be a debit balance on the bank statement and a debit balance in the cash book.	✓
At the year end, the balance on the bank statement will be included in the trial balance.	

(c)

	True	False
A payment omitted from the cash book and not included in the bank statement is an example of a timing difference.		✓
A timing difference will always increase the cash book balance.		✓
If uncleared lodgements have been identified when performing a bank reconciliation, the cash book will not need to be updated.	✓	

TASK 4 (12 MARKS)

(a)

Cash Book

Date	Details	Bank	Date	Cheque	Details	Bank
01 April	Balance b/d	18,000	01 April	120045	Mose Ltd	6,234
19 April	Wallace	5,321	01 April	120046	Sabre	1,632
28 April	Bennett	685	01 April	120047	Hannan	41
29 April	Lewis	282	02 April	120048	Flinderson	4,444
4 April	Priceright	342	02 April	120049	Bratton	542
			08 April	120050	Falcon	432
			08 April	120051	Vickers	1,698
			14 April	DD	Steering Ltd	2,878
			14 April	DD	Steamcar	2,865
			29 April		Bank charges	54
			29 April		Overdraft fee	27
			30 April		Balance c/d	3,783
		24,630				24,630
1 May	Balance b/d	3,783				

(b)

Balance per bank statement	£5,056
Outstanding lodgements	
Name: Bennett	£685
Name: Lewis	£282
Unpresented cheques	
Name: Bratton	£542
Name: Vickers	£1,698
Balance as per cash book	£3,783

TASK 5 (10 MARKS)

(a)

	✓
Rayyan made a payment of VAT to HMR&C and recorded this transaction in the journal.	
Zein has a receivable which has been outstanding for two months and wishes to make an allowance for a doubtful debt. Zein recorded the increase in the allowance for doubtful debts in the journal.	✓
Nour incurred bank fees and charges. The fees and charges were recorded in the journal.	
Farah calculated the annual depreciation charge on the delivery van used in the business. The depreciation charge was recorded in the journal.	✓

(b) £9,959

Payroll liabilities – HMRC

Details	Amount £	Details	Amount £
Balance b/d	85	Employer NI	2,900
		Employee NI	3,419
Balance c/d	9,959	PAYE	3,725
	10,044		**10,044**
		Balance b/d	9,959

(c)

Account name	Debit £	Credit £
Non-current asset	4,000	
VAT	850	
Repairs and maintenance	250	
Payable		5,100

TASK 6 (10 MARKS)

(a)

	✓
If the value of a transaction was transposed from £963 to £693 when both the debit and credit entries were posted into the ledger accounts, this not will require a suspense account to be opened.	✓
A suspense account is used to record accounting for the depreciation expense for the year.	
If the totals of the trial balance do not agree, one possible reason for this will be that a ledger balance has been omitted.	✓
A suspense account will normally be part of the initial trial balance for a business at the start of the accounting year.	

(b)

Error in the general ledger	Error disclosed by the trial balance ✓	Error NOT disclosed by the trial balance ✓
Recording a bank payment for purchases on the debit side of both the bank and purchases account.	✓	
Recording a payment for rent and rates in a non-current assets account.		✓

(c)   (i)   **What is the balance on the suspense account in the trial balance?**   (2 marks)

£26	Credit

The trial balance has a debit total (£57,636) larger than its credit total (£57,610), which means we need a credit balance in suspense to balance the trial balance. This credit balance is £26 (£57,636 – £57,610).

This can be proved when we clear the suspense using the journals in part (ii).

Suspense

Details	Amount £	Details	Amount £
Profit on sale of van	350	Balance b/d	26
		VAT	324
	350		350

(ii)

Error 1 Account name	£	Debit ✓	Credit ✓
VAT	324	✓	
Suspense	324		✓
Error 2 Account name			
Suspense	350	✓	
Profit on disposal of van	350		✓

TASK 7   (10 MARKS)

(a)

Receivables ledger control

Details	Amount £	Details	Amount £
Balance b/d	5,750	Sales returns	345
Sales	12,450	Bank	8,234
		Discounts allowed	32
		Contra with payables ledger control	1,950
		Irrecoverable debts	940
		Balance c/d	6,699

HMRC – tax and insurance liabilities

Details	Amount £	Details	Amount £
Balance b/d	75	PAYE	1,345
Bank	3,450	Employer NI	1,128
Balance c/d	156	Employee NI	1,208

Payables ledger control

Details	Amount £	Details	Amount £
Purchases returns	827	Balance b/d	4,345
Discounts received	252	Purchases	8,450
Bank	4,273		
Contra with receivables ledger control	1,950		
Balance c/d	5,493		

Repairs and maintenance

Details	Amount £	Details	Amount £
Bank	365		
Bank	142		
Petty cash	13	Balance c/d	520

(b)

Balances at 31 October	Debit £	Credit £
Sales		14,450
Purchases	8,450	
Admin expenses	1,209	
Irrecoverable debt expense	940	
Payables ledger control account		5,493
Repairs and maintenance	520	
Capital account		6,638
Inventory	3,268	
Receivables ledger control account	6,699	
Discounts received		252
Bank	1,923	
HMRC – tax and insurance liabilities		156
Wages expense	8,980	
Bank loan		5,000
Totals	31,989	31,989

TASK 8 (10 MARKS)

Suspense

Details	Amount £	Details	Amount £
Balance from TB	1,835	Receivables ledger control	3,725
General expenses	1,890		
	3,725		3,725

Trial Balance as at 31 December	Dr £	Cr £
Sales		279,082
Purchases	183,593	
Opening inventory	21,211	
Payroll expenses	61,326	
General expenses (24,790–1890)	22,900	
Capital account		15,710
Receivables ledger control (22,642+3,725)	26,367	
Payables ledger control		15,566
Bank		2,510
VAT		2,529
Total	**315,397**	**315,397**